Sermon on the Mount

Adopted Into a Kingdom

Angela Lee

Table of Contents

The Plan for This Study

This study is based on the Observation, Interpretation, and Application method of Bible study. The questions and commentary are designed to help you move through these steps:

Observation: What does the text say?
Read the entire text for comprehension.
Read again and consider: Who was this written to? What is happening in the passage? When and where did this take place? Why did the author write this?
Mark any key words, repeated phrases, or ideas.
Notice transition words. (Therefore, then, for, so, after, etc.)
Notice any lists, contrasts, comparisons, or types of imagery used.

Interpretation: What does the text mean?
Consult different translations.
Look up cross-references.
What would the original hearers have thought?
How does this passage fit into the greater story of the Bible? (Creation-Fall-Redemption-New Creation)
Paraphrase: Rewrite the text in your own words.
Consult reliable commentaries.

Application: How do I apply it to my life?
What does this passage tell us about God?
What does this passage tell you about your sin and your need for a Savior?
Is there a command to obey? A promise to claim?
How might this truth transform my life and perspective today?

Introduction
Background, Purpose, and Themes

Observation & Interpretation

1. First, it will help us to understand the context of the Sermon on the Mount within Matthew. Read the following passages from Matthew 1-4 and consider the ways Matthew introduces Jesus. Underline what you learn about Jesus, His character, and His origins from these passages.

Matthew 1

1 This is the genealogy[a] of Jesus the Messiah[b] the son of David,the son of Abraham:

2 Abraham was the father of Isaac,
   Isaac the father of Jacob,
   Jacob the father of Judah and his brothers,
   3 Judah the father of Perez and Zerah, whose mother was Tamar,
   Perez the father of Hezron,
   Hezron the father of Ram,
   4 Ram the father of Amminadab,
   Amminadab the father of Nahshon,
   Nahshon the father of Salmon,
   5 Salmon the father of Boaz, whose mother was Rahab,
   Boaz the father of Obed, whose mother was Ruth,
   Obed the father of Jesse,
   6 and Jesse the father of King David.
David was the father of Solomon, whose mother had been Uriah's
      wife,

⁷ Solomon the father of Rehoboam,
Rehoboam the father of Abijah,
Abijah the father of Asa,
⁸ Asa the father of Jehoshaphat,
Jehoshaphat the father of Jehoram,
Jehoram the father of Uzziah,
⁹ Uzziah the father of Jotham,
Jotham the father of Ahaz,
Ahaz the father of Hezekiah,
¹⁰ Hezekiah the father of Manasseh,
Manasseh the father of Amon,
Amon the father of Josiah,
¹¹ and Josiah the father of Jeconiah[c] and his brothers at the time
of the exile to Babylon.
¹² After the exile to Babylon:
Jeconiah was the father of Shealtiel,
Shealtiel the father of Zerubbabel,
¹³ Zerubbabel the father of Abihud,
Abihud the father of Eliakim,
Eliakim the father of Azor,
¹⁴ Azor the father of Zadok,
Zadok the father of Akim,
Akim the father of Elihud,
¹⁵ Elihud the father of Eleazar,
Eleazar the father of Matthan,
Matthan the father of Jacob,
¹⁶ and Jacob the father of Joseph, the husband of Mary, and Mary
was the mother of Jesus who is called the Messiah.

¹⁷ Thus there were fourteen generations in all from Abraham to
David, fourteen from David to the exile to Babylon, and fourteen
from the exile to the Messiah.

¹⁸ This is how the birth of Jesus the Messiah came about: His mother
Mary was pledged to be married to Joseph, but before they came
together, she was found to be pregnant through the Holy
Spirit.¹⁹ Because Joseph her husband was faithful to the law, and yet

did not want to expose her to public disgrace, he had in mind to divorce her quietly.

²⁰ But after he had considered this, an angel of the Lord appeared to him in a dream and said, "Joseph son of David, do not be afraid to take Mary home as your wife, because what is conceived in her is from the Holy Spirit. ²¹ She will give birth to a son, and you are to give him the name Jesus, because he will save his people from their sins."

²² All this took place to fulfill what the Lord had said through the prophet: ²³ "The virgin will conceive and give birth to a son, and they will call him Immanuel" (which means "God with us").

²⁴ When Joseph woke up, he did what the angel of the Lord had commanded him and took Mary home as his wife. ²⁵ But he did not consummate their marriage until she gave birth to a son. And he gave him the name Jesus.

Chapter 2

2 After Jesus was born in Bethlehem in Judea, during the time of King Herod, Magi from the east came to Jerusalem ² and asked, "Where is the one who has been born king of the Jews? We saw his star when it rose and have come to worship him."

³ When King Herod heard this he was disturbed, and all Jerusalem with him. ⁴ When he had called together all the people's chief priests and teachers of the law, he asked them where the Messiah was to be born. ⁵ "In Bethlehem in Judea," they replied, "for this is what the prophet has written:

⁶ "'But you, Bethlehem, in the land of Judah,
    are by no means least among the rulers of Judah;
for out of you will come a ruler
    who will shepherd my people Israel.'"
⁷ Then Herod called the Magi secretly and found out from them the exact time the star had appeared. ⁸ He sent them to Bethlehem and

said, "Go and search carefully for the child. As soon as you find him, report to me, so that I too may go and worship him."

⁹ After they had heard the king, they went on their way, and the star they had seen when it rose went ahead of them until it stopped over the place where the child was. ¹⁰ When they saw the star, they were overjoyed. ¹¹ On coming to the house, they saw the child with his mother Mary, and they bowed down and worshiped him. Then they opened their treasures and presented him with gifts of gold, frankincense and myrrh. ¹² And having been warned in a dream not to go back to Herod, they returned to their country by another route.

¹³ When they had gone, an angel of the Lord appeared to Joseph in a dream. "Get up," he said, "take the child and his mother and escape to Egypt. Stay there until I tell you, for Herod is going to search for the child to kill him."

¹⁴ So he got up, took the child and his mother during the night and left for Egypt, ¹⁵ where he stayed until the death of Herod. And so was fulfilled what the Lord had said through the prophet: "Out of Egypt I called my son."

¹⁶ When Herod realized that he had been outwitted by the Magi, he was furious, and he gave orders to kill all the boys in Bethlehem and its vicinity who were two years old and under, in accordance with the time he had learned from the Magi. ¹⁷ Then what was said through the prophet Jeremiah was fulfilled:

¹⁸ "A voice is heard in Ramah,
    weeping and great mourning,
Rachel weeping for her children
    and refusing to be comforted,
    because they are no more."

¹⁹ After Herod died, an angel of the Lord appeared in a dream to Joseph in Egypt ²⁰ and said, "Get up, take the child and his mother

and go to the land of Israel, for those who were trying to take the child's life are dead."

21 So he got up, took the child and his mother and went to the land of Israel. 22 But when he heard that Archelaus was reigning in Judea in place of his father Herod, he was afraid to go there. Having been warned in a dream, he withdrew to the district of Galilee, 23 and he went and lived in a town called Nazareth. So was fulfilled what was said through the prophets, that he would be called a Nazarene.

Matthew 3:13-17

13 Then Jesus came from Galilee to the Jordan to be baptized by John. 14 But John tried to deter him, saying, "I need to be baptized by you, and do you come to me?"

15 Jesus replied, "Let it be so now; it is proper for us to do this to fulfill all righteousness." Then John consented.

16 As soon as Jesus was baptized, he went up out of the water. At that moment heaven was opened, and he saw the Spirit of God descending like a dove and alighting on him. 17 And a voice from heaven said, "This is my Son, whom I love; with him I am well pleased."

Matthew 4:1-17

Then Jesus was led by the Spirit into the wilderness to be tempted by the devil. Then Jesus was led by the Spirit into the wilderness to be tempted by the devil. 2 After fasting forty days and forty nights, he was hungry. 3 The tempter came to him and said, "If you are the Son of God, tell these stones to become bread."

4 Jesus answered, "It is written: 'Man shall not live on bread alone, but on every word that comes from the mouth of God.'"

5 Then the devil took him to the holy city and had him stand on the highest point of the temple. 6 "If you are the Son of God," he said, "throw yourself down. For it is written:

"'He will command his angels concerning you,
 and they will lift you up in their hands,
 so that you will not strike your foot against a stone.'[c]"
[7] Jesus answered him, "It is also written: 'Do not put the Lord your God to the test.'[d]"

[8] Again, the devil took him to a very high mountain and showed him all the kingdoms of the world and their splendor. [9] "All this I will give you," he said, "if you will bow down and worship me."

[10] Jesus said to him, "Away from me, Satan! For it is written: 'Worship the Lord your God, and serve him only.'"

[11] Then the devil left him, and angels came and attended him.

[12] When Jesus heard that John had been put in prison, he withdrew to Galilee. [13] Leaving Nazareth, he went and lived in Capernaum, which was by the lake in the area of Zebulun and Naphtali— [14] to fulfill what was said through the prophet Isaiah:

[15] "Land of Zebulun and land of Naphtali,
 the Way of the Sea, beyond the Jordan,
 Galilee of the Gentiles—
[16] the people living in darkness
 have seen a great light;
on those living in the land of the shadow of death
 a light has dawned."
[17] From that time on Jesus began to preach, "Repent, for the kingdom of heaven has come near."

Matthew 4:23-25

[23] Jesus went throughout Galilee, teaching in their synagogues, proclaiming the good news of the kingdom, and healing every disease and sickness among the people. [24] News about him spread all over Syria, and people brought to him all who were ill with various diseases, those suffering severe pain, the demon-possessed, those having seizures, and the paralyzed; and he healed

them. ²⁵ Large crowds from Galilee, the Decapolis, Jerusalem, Judea and the region across the Jordan followed him.

What did you learn from this exercise? What questions do you have about Matthew 1-4?

2. Read **Matthew 5:1-2**; these verses introduce the Sermon on the Mount.

¹ Now when Jesus saw the crowds, he went up on a mountainside and sat down. His disciples came to him, ² and he began to teach them.

Who is speaking? To whom are they speaking?

Commentary

Who wrote the Sermon on the Mount? To whom is it written?

The Sermon on the Mount is recorded in the book of Matthew. Matthew wrote his gospel, a record of Jesus' life and teaching, primarily to a Jewish audience.

What is the context of the Sermon on the Mount within Matthew?

Matthew's aim was to convince the Jews that Jesus is their long-awaited Messiah. In doing so, he recorded the life and ministry of Christ to prove that Jesus is the true David and the true Moses: two revered figures among the Jewish people.

In the first four chapters of Matthew, he explains that:
- *Jesus is the true, Davidic King of Bethlehem.* Matthew 1 details Jesus' genealogy. He is the promised Son of David, whose birth, as recorded in Matthew 2, fulfilled the prophecy of the Messiah in Micah 5:2 and Isaiah 7:14. Matthew's audience would have identified the role of king with one who was to not only enforce the law, but also to embody the law. This is significant as we study the Sermon on the Mount. Matthew reminds us that Jesus is the true and only Davidic King who embodied the law of God perfectly.

-Jesus is the true deliverer and lawgiver, Moses. Moses passed through the waters of the Red Sea in Exodus 14, providing deliverance for God's people; and Matthew records that Jesus passed through the waters of baptism in Matthew 3, as God's voice declared from the heavens that Jesus was the one His people should follow for deliverance (Matthew 3:17). Moses was tested in the wilderness in Exodus 15-18, and Jesus overcame Satan's temptation in the desert in Matthew 4.

Moses was known by the Jews as the one who gave the law, but Deuteronomy 18:15-20 prophesied of a greater lawgiver. We remember that Moses ascended Mount Sinai in Exodus 19 to receive the law from God. And finally, on a different mountain in Matthew 5, we read that Jesus ascended and sat down to give laws and guidelines for His Kingdom.

Matthew sets us up in Matthew 1-4 to worship Jesus as the one who fulfills Matthew 5-7. In Matthew 5-7, Jesus gave instructions for God's Kingdom as the greater lawgiver, the promised deliverer, and the King. This message is known as the Sermon on the Mount.

What is the purpose of the Sermon on the Mount?

The sermon is thought to be a manual on being a follower of Christ. Matthew divided his gospel into 5 sections. Each section consists of a narrative of Jesus' life and works and ends with a discourse- or a recording of Jesus' teaching on a specific topic. Matthew 5-7, the Sermon on the Mount, is known as the "discipleship discourse" (ESV Study Bible).

"Up on the mountain," Jesus, having just called His disciples, taught them how to be His followers in the new Kingdom. His instruction in the sermon reflected His message in Matthew 4:17, "Repent! for the Kingdom of heaven is at hand." God's people had always been called to be set apart from the rest of the world. Israel was told, "You are to be holy to me because I, the LORD, am holy, and I have set you apart from the nations to be my own."(Leviticus 20:26). In the Sermon on the Mount, Jesus spoke of what this kind of "set apartness" would look like for His followers. He explained how to turn in repentance, be separate from the ways of the world, and be a disciple of Christ in God's Kingdom.

Themes We Will Focus On

Jesus is our righteousness, the One who obeyed God perfectly.

Jesus calls His disciples to an obedience to Him that comes from the heart. A quick read through of the sermon shows us that this obedience is not something we can accomplish on our own. John Stott sums it up this way, "Only a belief in the necessity and possibility of a new birth can keep us from reading the Sermon on the Mount with either foolish optimism or hopeless despair" (Stott, 29). Jesus gave these instructions in the Sermon on the Mount knowing they are only possible to apply through the good news of His own life, death, and resurrection.

Second Corinthians 5:21 says, "For our sake he made him to be sin who knew no sin, so that in him we might become the righteousness of God."

Romans 5:1-2, 5 says, "Therefore, since we have been justified by faith, we have peace with God through our Lord Jesus Christ. Through him we have also obtained access by faith into this grace in which we stand, and we rejoice in hope of the glory of God... and hope does not put us to shame, because God's love has been poured into our hearts through the Holy Spirit who has been given to us."

Our hope for living the Sermon on the Mount is in our reliance on Christ. If we trust in His perfect obedience, He has justified us by His work on the cross; He has given us His Spirit so that we can walk in obedience as His followers.

Jesus is God's true Son, who teaches us to live in light of our adoption.
Romans 8:15-17 says, "For you did not receive the spirit of slavery to fall back into fear, but you have received the Spirit of adoption as Sons, by whom we cry, 'Abba! Father!' The Spirit Himself bears witness with our spirit that we are the children of God."

The Holy Spirit is "a spirit of adoption"; when He grants us new hearts through His work on the cross, He also makes us His children. One perspective of the Sermon on the Mount is that Jesus is teaching us how to operate in the family of God as dependent children, living in light of our Father's love and care.

J.I Packer wrote, "...just as the knowledge of His unique Sonship controlled Jesus' living of His own life, so he insists that that knowledge of our adoptive sonship must control our lives too. This comes out in his teaching again and again, but nowhere more clearly that the Sermon on the Mount" (Packer, 210). The Sermon on the Mount calls God's children to reflect their Father's likeness and live as those who belong to Him.

In this study, we will explore how our adoption into the family of God, by His spirit, frees us to pursue obedience and experience the blessing described in the Sermon on the Mount. As we study our Heavenly Father's heart and watch our brother, Jesus' example, we will study how to live filled with the Holy Spirit as we worship as Christ's disciples in the family of God.

Application & Reflection

1. Repentance can be defined as: a turning away from sin and turning to God. The Sermon is part of Jesus' message to, "Repent, for the Kingdom of heaven is at hand" (Matthew 4:17). How does this inform our view of the teaching?

2. What does it mean to you that if you know Christ, God has adopted you as His son or daughter?

3. One angle of Matthew 5-7 is that it teaches us how to live out our adoption into God's kingdom. How will this inform your time studying the sermon?

Lesson 2
The Beatitudes
Matthew 5:3–5

Observation & Interpretation

Read Matthew 5:3-5 and consider the following questions.

[3] "Blessed are the poor in spirit,
  for theirs is the kingdom of heaven.
[4] Blessed are those who mourn,
  for they will be comforted.
[5] Blessed are the meek,
  for they will inherit the earth.

[6] "Blessed are those who hunger and thirst for righteousness, for they shall be satisfied.

[7] "Blessed are the merciful, for they shall receive mercy.

[8] "Blessed are the pure in heart, for they shall see God.

[9] "Blessed are the peacemakers, for they shall be called sons[a] of God.

[10] "Blessed are those who are persecuted for righteousness' sake, for theirs is the kingdom of heaven.

[11] "Blessed are you when others revile you and persecute you and utter all kinds of evil against you falsely on my account. [12] Rejoice and be glad, for your reward is great in heaven, for so they persecuted the prophets who were before you.

1. List the rewards in the second part of each verse as explained in verses 3-12.
Ex: Blessed are the poor in spirit, [for theirs is the kingdom of heaven.]

2. As you consider the rewards Jesus mentioned for each character trait, what do you think the word 'blessed' means as Jesus used it?

3. Read **Psalm 86:1-5**, **Isaiah 57:15,** and **Isaiah 61:1-11** with attention to the concepts of "poor in spirit" and "mourning." Jesus used language from these passages in Matthew 5:3-5. Underline phrases that remind you of this mourning and also the blessing and rescue that is promised.

Psalm 86:1-5

[1] Hear me, Lord, and answer me,
  for I am poor and needy.
[2] Guard my life, for I am faithful to you;
  save your servant who trusts in you.
You are my God; [3] have mercy on me, Lord,
  for I call to you all day long.
[4] Bring joy to your servant, Lord,
  for I put my trust in you.
[5] You, Lord, are forgiving and good,
  abounding in love to all who call to you.

Isaiah 57:15

[15] For this is what the high and exalted One says—
  he who lives forever, whose name is holy:

"I live in a high and holy place,
  but also with the one who is contrite and lowly in spirit,
to revive the spirit of the lowly
  and to revive the heart of the contrite.

Isaiah 61:1-11

The Spirit of the Sovereign Lord is on me,
  because the Lord has anointed me
  to proclaim good news to the poor.
He has sent me to bind up the brokenhearted,
  to proclaim freedom for the captives
  and release from darkness for the prisoners,[a]
2 to proclaim the year of the Lord's favor
  and the day of vengeance of our God,
to comfort all who mourn,
3 and provide for those who grieve in Zion—
to bestow on them a crown of beauty
  instead of ashes,
the oil of joy
  instead of mourning,
and a garment of praise
  instead of a spirit of despair.
They will be called oaks of righteousness,
  a planting of the Lord
  for the display of his splendor.
4 They will rebuild the ancient ruins
  and restore the places long devastated;
they will renew the ruined cities
  that have been devastated for generations.
5 Strangers will shepherd your flocks;
  foreigners will work your fields and vineyards.
6 And you will be called priests of the Lord,
  you will be named ministers of our God.
You will feed on the wealth of nations,
  and in their riches you will boast.

⁷ Instead of your shame
  you will receive a double portion,
and instead of disgrace
  you will rejoice in your inheritance.
And so you will inherit a double portion in your land,
  and everlasting joy will be yours.
⁸ "For I, the Lord, love justice;
  I hate robbery and wrongdoing.
In my faithfulness I will reward my people
  and make an everlasting covenant with them.
⁹ Their descendants will be known among the nations
  and their offspring among the peoples.
All who see them will acknowledge
  that they are a people the Lord has blessed."
¹⁰ I delight greatly in the Lord;
  my soul rejoices in my God.
For he has clothed me with garments of salvation
  and arrayed me in a robe of his righteousness,
as a bridegroom adorns his head like a priest,
  and as a bride adorns herself with her jewels.
¹¹ For as the soil makes the sprout come up
  and a garden causes seeds to grow,
so the Sovereign Lord will make righteousness
  and praise spring up before all nations.

How do these passages help us understand Matthew 5:3-5 and the blessing promised?

4. Look up Matthew 5:5 in different translations. How can poverty in spirit and mourning over sin (vs 3-4) lead to meekness?

Commentary

In Isaiah 61, Israel was poor, broken-hearted, and in mourning over their sin. Isaiah prophesied of a Messiah in this chapter, one who would bring "good news to the poor," "bind up the broken hearted," and "comfort all who mourn." In Luke 4:18-19, Jesus quoted this prophecy and said it was talking about Him; the saving, healing, redeeming Messiah had come. Jesus shared the implications of this in Matthew 5:3-5. He came to bring blessings to the children of God through their poverty in spirit, their mourning over sin, and their dependence on Him.

Through the coming of Christ, the Messiah, those in the Messianic Kingdom are marked by specific character traits and blessings. These are listed in Chapter 5:3-12 in what are often called the "Beatitudes."

Verse 3

"Poor in spirit" refers to those who know their true spiritual condition. The NLT translates this phrase as "poor and realize their need for Him." They are blessed because they hope in God's redemption alone, and God's redemption in Christ is full and complete. As John Stott says, "All they could do is cry out for mercy, and He heard their cry" (40). Just as the tax collector in Luke 18:9-14 cried, "Lord, have mercy on me, a sinner"; when we acknowledge our spiritual bankruptcy and depend on Christ alone, "our citizenship is in heaven." (Philippians 3:20).

Verse 4

When we are aware of our poverty in spirit, we mourn over our sin. We are granted a "godly grief" leading to repentance (2 Cor 7:10).

In Psalm 119:136 David said, "My eyes shed streams of water, because they do not keep your law." When we are given the Holy Spirit, we mourn over our own sin and the sin of the world. But God comforts these righteous tears through Christ. Jesus knew His audience. He was speaking to His disciples along with others who had gathered to listen, and nearly all of them would know of the hard and grief-filled history of wayward Israel. Whether it was mourning over sin that led them to exile, or mourning the many layers of loss that came with the fallen world, Jesus intimately knew the sorrows and despair of His people. He didn't offer this announcement of blessing tritely. The Old Testament prophets had declared that "Comforter" was to be one of the offices of the Messiah. Isaiah 61:3-4 explains that those who mourn will receive "a beautiful headdress instead of ashes, the oil of gladness instead of mourning, the garment of praise instead of a faint spirit..." Matthew 5:4 declares: this Comforter Messiah has come! Jesus meets us in our grief with comfort.

At the cross, though there is mourning over sin and its cost, the resurrection "turns our sorrow to joy" (John 16:20-22). Through Christ, God is making all things new, and one day we will experience final, full restoration and comfort (Revelation 21:1-5).

Verse 5

When we are aware of our spiritual condition as needy, helpless, and sinful, our posture before God and others is "meek." Some translations say "gentle" or "humble."

The Message paraphrases Matthew 5:5a, "You're blessed when you're content with just who you are—no more, no less." The meek have accepted what God says about who they are, "poor in spirit" and in need of mercy. Dr Martin Lloyd Jones wrote, "Meekness is essentially a true view of oneself, expressing itself in attitude and conduct with respect to others" (Qtd. Stott, 43).

The meek don't try to act as if they are better than they are, but they live honestly as dependent, loved children of their Heavenly Father. They are not defensive over their own righteousness, but dependent and strong in Christ's righteousness.

The next part of the verse is so backward and beautiful. The meek are blessed because they will "inherit the earth." This is the opposite group of people of whom you would think would "inherit the earth." It's not the ones fighting for more that they deserve, the angry, aggressive, or the strong that will conquer and receive the earth. It's the meek. The ones who rely, not on themselves, but on the strength and righteousness of Jesus. They don't run in with a conquering posture but they trust they are "more than conquerors" through Christ, and He will one day indeed inherit the earth. They don't grasp at privileges or inheritances that they don't deserve, but they trust in the Christ-secured inheritance of a new heaven and earth (Revelation 22:1).

Christ is the perfect example of this kind of heart. Jesus' meekness was different from ours—it didn't flow from the awareness of his sin. Jesus never sinned; He had every right to be proud- but He chose meekness, humility, and gentleness. "Though he was in the form of God, he did not count equality with God a thing to be grasped, but He emptied Himself, by taking on the form of a servant" (Philippians 2:6). His posture reflected gentle servanthood, and He described Himself as "gentle and lowly in heart" (Matthew 11:29). When we acknowledge our poverty in spirit and our need for mercy, we encounter the meek and humble heart of Christ. As we rest in and turn our eyes to His heart, He will change our hearts to be like His.

Application & Reflection

1. How is the person who is "blessed" in Matthew 5:1-5 different than the person the world tends to think of as "blessed?"

2. Which character trait of a believer and corresponding blessing encourages you? Which one is challenging to you?

3. How have you experienced one or more of the "blessings" described in Matthew 5:3-5?

What did this experience teach you about God and His Kingdom?

Lesson 3
The Beatitudes

Matthew 5:6–12

Observation & Interpretation

Read Matthew 5:6–12 and consider the following questions.

[6] Blessed are those who hunger and thirst for righteousness,
  for they will be filled.
[7] Blessed are the merciful,
  for they will be shown mercy.
[8] Blessed are the pure in heart,
  for they will see God.
[9] Blessed are the peacemakers,
  for they will be called children of God.
[10] Blessed are those who are persecuted because of righteousness,
  for theirs is the kingdom of heaven.
[11] "Blessed are you when people insult you, persecute you and falsely say all kinds of evil against you because of me. [12] Rejoice and be glad, because great is your reward in heaven, for in the same way they persecuted the prophets who were before you.

1. The following verses include similar concepts to those addressed in Jesus's beatitudes. Read the passages and then write the corresponding beatitude in your own words:

Matthew 6:33
[33] But seek first the kingdom of God and his righteousness, and all these things will be added to you.

Isaiah 55:1-2
[1] "Come, everyone who thirsts,
  come to the waters;
and he who has no money,
  come, buy and eat!
Come, buy wine and milk
  without money and without price.
[2] Why do you spend your money for that which is not bread,
  and your labor for that which does not satisfy?
Listen diligently to me, and eat what is good,
  and delight yourselves in rich food.

Revelation 7:17

For the Lamb in the midst of the throne will be their shepherd,
  and he will guide them to springs of living water,
and God will wipe away every tear from their eyes.

Write Matthew 5:6 in your own words:

Matthew 25:34-36

Then the King will say to those on his right, 'Come, you who are blessed by my Father, inherit the kingdom prepared for you from the foundation of the world. [35] For I was hungry and you gave me food, I was thirsty and you gave me drink, I was a stranger and you welcomed me, [36] I was naked and you clothed me, I was sick and you visited me, I was in prison and you came to me.'

Ephesians 4:32

[32] Be kind to one another, tenderhearted, forgiving one another, as God in Christ forgave you.

Write Matthew 5:7 in your own words:

Psalm 24:4-5

[4] He who has clean hands and a pure heart,
 who does not lift up his soul to what is false
 and does not swear deceitfully.
[5] He will receive blessing from the Lord
 and righteousness from the God of his salvation.

1 John 3:2-3
[2] Beloved, we are God's children now, and what we will be has not yet appeared; but we know that when he appears we shall be like him, because we shall see him as he is. [3] And everyone who thus hopes in him purifies himself as he is pure.

Write Matthew 5:8 in your own words:

Romans 5:1-2

Therefore, since we have been justified by faith, we have peace with God through our Lord Jesus Christ. ² Through him we have also obtained access by faith into this grace in which we stand, and we rejoice in hope of the glory of God.

Isaiah 9:6

For to us a child is born,
 to us a son is given;
and the government shall be upon his shoulder,
 and his name shall be called
Wonderful Counselor, Mighty God,
 Everlasting Father, Prince of Peace.

John 1:12

¹² But to all who did receive him, who believed in his name, he gave the right to become children of God,

Write Matthew 5:9 in your own words:

1 Peter 4:14
¹⁴ If you are insulted for the name of Christ, you are blessed, because the Spirit of glory and of God rests upon you.

Hebrews 11:24-27

²⁴ By faith Moses, when he was grown up, refused to be called the son of Pharaoh's daughter, ²⁵ choosing rather to be mistreated with the people of God than to enjoy the fleeting pleasures of sin.

26 He considered the reproach of Christ greater wealth than the treasures of Egypt, for he was looking to the reward. **27** By faith he left Egypt, not being afraid of the anger of the king, for he endured as seeing him who is invisible.

Write Matthew 5:10-11 in your own words:

2. Considering these interpretations, explain a few ways the beatitudes relate to one another (ex: how does receiving mercy lead us to being a peacemaker?).

Commentary

Verse 6

"*Righteousness*- in the dictionary is defined as 'behavior that is morally justifiable or right.' This behavior is characterized by accepted standards of morality, justice, virtue, or uprightness. The Bible's standard of human righteousness is God's own perfection in every attribute, every attitude, every behavior, and every word. Thus, God's laws, as given in the Bible, both describe His own character and constitute the plumb line by which He measures human righteousness" (Got Questions, 2020).

Jesus acknowledged that as we live out the first steps of the beatitudes: becoming poor in spirit, mourning over the cost of sin, and humility, we will realize our lack of righteousness (both in our hearts and in our world) and it will lead us to "hunger and thirst" for the righteousness of God. Some scholars have interpreted this beatitude about righteousness to mean justice, when God will right every wrong. Some people have interpreted the righteousness as personal righteousness, as in growing in purity and obedience to God's perfect and right standard in His word. It's also likely that it could be both. Pursuing personal dependence on Christ's righteousness will lead us to do right and pursue justice.

When the pain of mourning over sin fades and we have space for reflection, a hunger wells up in us. As we behold Him and His righteousness in His word, our self-righteousness and shallow perception of justice fades, and we long for the real thing. He carves in our hearts a hunger for God's word, God's will, and a thirst for His Spirit.

As our example, Jesus lived His life being filled by the food of "doing the will of Him who sent [Him]" (John 4:34). And to those who receive Him, He promises "living water... whoever drinks of the water [He] will give him will never be thirsty again" (John 4:14).

As we seek and behold His righteous character through His word, we will be awed, led to repentance, changed, and satisfied. We'll be satisfied here on earth as we experience His perfection and goodness, and we'll be satisfied in heaven when all is right and just.

Verse 7

Mercy can be defined as compassion for people in need, and need comes in various forms. Whether our pain and need comes from our own personal sin or flows from the fallenness of the world, our merciful God bends down to meet us where we are. He sends mercy through forgiveness, through people, and through His presence and word (to only name a few ways). Though we were dead, "God, being rich in *mercy,* because of His great love with which He loved us, even when we were dead in our trespasses, made us alive together with Christ." (Ephesians 2:4-5). He restores us and comes near to broken hearts.

If we have believed in Christ, we have received mercy, and as we are moved and humbled by His selfless mercy, we become merciful. Through Christ, God has not given us what we deserve; he doesn't leave us in the pit. Knowing this mercy leads us to extend mercy to others who, like us, are in desperate need of mercy. Those who have received the mercy of Christ are marked by their merciful acts toward others.
Sinclair Ferguson said, "Mercy involves getting down on your hands and knees and doing what you can to restore dignity to someone whose life has been broken by sin..." (Akin, 10). This mercy involves forgiveness of others' sins (Ephesians 4:32), and loving, restoring care for the whole person in need.

Verse 8

John Stott helps us see that in this Beatitude, the pure in heart are the ones who are "utterly sincere" (49). Psalm 24:3-4 says, "who shall ascend the hill of the Lord?... he who has clean hands and a pure heart, and who does not lift up his soul to what is false." The motives of the pure in heart are open and unhidden from God and men—they don't have secret motives or agendas.

Though we were created to worship God in single-hearted purity, our hearts are fallen and our worship is disordered (Genesis 1-3). But Jesus came to give hope, that though our hearts fail, we may be restored and "see God." Everyone who hopes in Christ and His mercy alone "purifies himself as He is pure" (1 John 3:3). We pursue and receive this pure heart by receiving His spirit and practicing repentance. When God gives us a new heart, we begin to "behold the glory of the Lord and be transformed from one degree of glory to another" (2 Cor 3:18). He allows us to see Him, and in turn, desire Him and seek Him more.

In Christ, God has plans to transform our hearts to the utter sincerity and purity of a child as He prepares us for our family reunion in heaven when we will see God face to face. 1 John 3:2-3 says, "But we know that when Christ appears, we shall be like him, for we shall see him as he is. All who have this hope in him purify themselves, just as he is pure." When we acknowledge our lack of purity and hope in His, our broken and tangled motives are purified and cleansed by the grace of Jesus, and He begins to change our hearts. Those who have this pure heart are blessed, and one day they will see Him as He is. One day we will see Him face to face in complete purity and perfect worship (Revelation 22:3-4).

Verse 9

God has made peace with us through the blood of the cross, reconciled us to Himself (Colossians 1:20), and adopted us into His family. When we hope in our brother, Jesus, the Prince of Peace (Isaiah 9:6), we have peace with the God of Peace (Romans 16:20.)

As we enter His family, we take on His family likeness and become peacemakers (Akin, 12). We now are able to offer peace to others as His ambassadors, as Paul says, "We implore you on Christ's behalf, be reconciled to God." When we are at peace with God, He leads us by His spirit to be at peace with one another.

We are blessed when we are peacemakers because it gives us a glimpse of the peace God has given us through Christ. As we extend this peace and forgiveness over and over again, we look more and more like Jesus, and more and more like a son of God.

Verses 10-12

Though Jesus calls His followers to be peacemakers, the message of peace with God through repentance leads to others "reviling, persecuting, and uttering all kinds of evil falsely on [His] account." His message calls for repentance (Matthew 4:17). A lifestyle and message that leads others to see their need for repentance will often be met with opposition. Second Timothy 3:12 says, "all who live a Godly life in Christ Jesus will be persecuted."

Jesus shared that this persecution "is on His account," or "whoever rejects you rejects [Him]" (Luke 10:16). He encouraged the persecuted to rejoice; they have a great reward in heaven and the affirmation that they are true disciples. They are in good company with the "prophets before them." Isaiah was ignored and rejected (Isaiah 6), Jeremiah was thrown into a pit (Jeremiah 38), and John the Baptist was beheaded (Matthew 14). In the face of persecution, Paul resolved to "share in His sufferings, becoming like Him in His death, that by any means possible I may obtain the resurrection from the dead." (Philippians 3) Matthew Henry notes, "the grace which was sufficient for them, to carry them through their sufferings, shall not be deficient for you." We too have this hope, grace, and promise of reward to carry us in the face of all kinds of persecution.

Application & Reflection

1. Is there a character trait or blessing described in these verses that you desire to grow in?

2. How will your desire to grow in this area inform your prayers?

3. How have you experienced one or more of the "blessings" described in the Beatitudes?

When you experienced this blessing, what did you learn from this about God and His Kingdom?

4. Read **Romans 8:9-16.** How can our adoption into God's family, and Jesus our brother's example give us hope for living out these beatitudes?

⁹ You, however, are not in the flesh but in the Spirit, if in fact the Spirit of God dwells in you. Anyone who does not have the Spirit of Christ does not belong to him. ¹⁰ But if Christ is in you, although the body is dead because of sin, the Spirit is life because of righteousness. ¹¹ If the Spirit of him who raised Jesus from the dead dwells in you, he who raised Christ Jesus from the dead will also give life to your mortal bodies through his Spirit who dwells in you.

¹² So then, brothers, we are debtors, not to the flesh, to live according to the flesh. ¹³ For if you live according to the flesh you will die, but if by the Spirit you put to death the deeds of the body, you will live. ¹⁴ For all who are led by the Spirit of God are sons of God.¹⁵ For you did not receive the spirit of slavery to fall back into fear, but you have received the Spirit of adoption as sons, by whom we cry, "Abba! Father!" ¹⁶ The Spirit himself bears witness with our spirit that we are children of God, ¹⁷ and if children, then heirs—heirs of God and fellow heirs with Christ, provided we suffer with him in order that we may also be glorified with him.

How can this hope spur you on today?

Lesson 4
Salt and Light
Matthew 5:13-16

Observation & Interpretation

Read Matthew 5:13-16 and consider the following questions.

[13] "You are the salt of the earth, but if salt has lost its taste, how shall its saltiness be restored? It is no longer good for anything except to be thrown out and trampled under people's feet.

[14] "You are the light of the world. A city set on a hill cannot be hidden.[15] Nor do people light a lamp and put it under a basket, but on a stand, and it gives light to all in the house. [16] In the same way, let your light shine before others, so that they may see your good works and give glory to your Father who is in heaven.

1. What word pictures did Jesus use to describe a Christian's role in the world?

What do you think is meant by this?

2. According to the text, when are salt and light NOT effective?

How do you think this relates to our witness as Christians?

3. What do you think is the connection between the Beatitudes and Jesus' statement about believers being salt and light for the world?

Commentary

As Jesus finished His description of a disciple's character (5:3-12), He began to share how living out these character traits should influence the world. He used word pictures of salt and light to describe the believer's purpose.

As believers carry out their roles as salt for a world dying of moral decay and light for a world trapped in darkness, the result will be "glory to [our] Father in heaven" (Matthew 5:16).

Verses 13-14

Jesus told His disciples that they were the salt of the earth. During Jesus' time, salt had many practical functions in everyday life. The two uses Jesus seemed to emphasize are preservation and purity.

Romans 8:19-23 provides insight on the decay and corruption of the world.

"... For the creation was subjected to futility, not willingly, but because of him who subjected it, in hope that the creation itself will be set free from its bondage to corruption and obtain the freedom of the glory of the children of God. For we know that the whole creation has been groaning together in the pains of childbirth until now. And not only the creation, but we ourselves, who have the firstfruits of the Spirit, groan inwardly as we wait eagerly for adoption as sons, the redemption of our bodies."

Paul described that the world experiences "eager longing," "bondage to corruption," and "groaning." The earth is in bondage to corruption, and its moral decay is inevitable. However, as Christians wait for the New Heaven and earth, we are filled with "the firstfruits" (Romans 8:23) of the Holy Spirit, in order to live out the call of the Beatitudes and reflect Christ to the world. When we do this, we, like salt as a preservative, will slow the decay of the earth.

In order for salt to be effective as a preservative for food, it has to remain pure. If it comes in contact with another substance and its makeup is changed, it is simply not salt anymore, and it's not functional. In the ancient world, when salt became impure and "lost its taste" it was no longer useful as a preservative and would be "thrown out" and used to fill the roads for people to walk on. Salt has to be pure to be salt, if it's not pure, it's not salt.

What makes us effective "salt" as a Christian is living genuinely and purely as children of God filled with His Holy Spirit. By His spirit we can live out the Beatitudes and be salt to the earth. Christ in us is what makes us salty. However, when we fail to walk by the Spirit and we walk impurely, we are ineffective, and we are useless in our role as salt to the world.

Verses 14-16

Isaiah 49:6 prophesied the Messiah as "a light for the nations, to be my salvation to the end of the earth." And later in His ministry, Jesus would confirm that He is "the light of the world" (John 8:14). Light against darkness had a rich background in the Old Testament. "It stood for revelation, instruction, hope, joy, righteousness, salvation, and the radiance of divine presence" (Akin, 19). As Jesus is the light, He explained that those who follow Him are also the light of the world. This is because of "Christ in us, the hope of Glory" (Colossians 1:27). When God adopts us into His family, we are filled with Christ so that we too are the light of the world.

The Message paraphrases 14-16, "You're here to be light, bringing out the God-colors in the world. God is not a secret to be kept. We're going public with this, as public as a city on a hill." Light in a dark place is visible to everyone. As we live out the Beatitudes and are filled with the Spirit of Christ, our life and deeds will be noticed. They, like a city on a hill made up of many shining lights, "cannot be hidden."

Jesus shared that the believer and the church are to have a profound effect on the spiritual darkness in the world. The dark shadows of pain and sin are to be exposed and illumined by Christ, through the light of His people and by the lamp of His word, so that the world might be alerted to the brightness and glory of our God. The light is to be seen. A "light under a basket," like salt without taste, is useless.

Why is the light in us to be seen? Not so that others might see us (Matthew 6:1), but our light is to shine before others so that our Father would be honored and praised. (16) The children of God, through Christ in them, are to shine as light to glorify their Father in heaven.

Application & Reflection

1. How have you experienced Jesus being a "light in darkness" in your own life?

How does this motivate you to be a light for others?

2. How have you seen the Church be light to the world and salt to the earth?

What did this experience teach you about God's Kingdom?

3. We lose our saltiness when we walk impurely, and our light fails to shine when we hide it. In your own life and/or in the life of your Christian community, what is keeping you from being useful as salt and light to those around you?

4. How will the call to be salt and light to those around you inform your prayers?

5. What is one way living out the Beatitudes before others could act as light that "gives glory to our Father in heaven?"

How can you live out this call this week?

Lesson 5
Understanding God's Word
Matthew 5:17-20

Observation & Interpretation

Read Matthew 5:17-20 and consider the following questions.

[17] "Do not think that I have come to abolish the Law or the Prophets; I have not come to abolish them but to fulfill them. [18] For truly, I say to you, until heaven and earth pass away, not an iota, not a dot, will pass from the Law until all is accomplished. [19] Therefore whoever relaxes one of the least of these commandments and teaches others to do the same will be called least in the kingdom of heaven, but whoever does them and teaches them will be called great in the kingdom of heaven. [20] For I tell you, unless your righteousness exceeds that of the scribes and Pharisees, you will never enter the kingdom of heaven.

1. What did Jesus believe about the Old Testament (the Law and the Prophets)?

2. Look up Matthew 5:18 in different translations. Describe in your own words what you think it means that Jesus came to "fulfill the law and prophets."

3. Read **John 5:39-40** and **Matthew 23:27-28**. In both passages, Jesus expands on the ways the righteousness of the Pharisees misses the mark.

John 5:39-40
[39] You search the Scriptures because you think that in them you have eternal life; and it is they that bear witness about me, [40] yet you refuse to come to me that you may have life.

Matthew 23:27-28
"Woe to you, scribes and Pharisees, hypocrites! For you are like whitewashed tombs, which outwardly appear beautiful, but within are full of dead people's bones and all uncleanness. [28] So you also outwardly appear righteous to others, but within you are full of hypocrisy and lawlessness.

Considering these passages alongside Matthew 5:17-20, how is the righteousness of the scribes and Pharisees different than the righteousness Jesus requires?

Commentary

In the rest of Chapter 5, we will study how Jesus clarifies some practical implications of living with a righteousness from the heart. In verses 17-20, He introduces this by clarifying how this righteousness relates with the "law and prophets," or what we know as the Old Testament.

Verse 17

Jesus had introduced a few new ideas in His ministry (John 7:46), but He clarified in verse 17 that there is no "break" with the Old Testament. He had not come to "abolish" the law and prophets; He came to fulfill them.

Jesus fills and completes the revelation of the character of God. God gave glimpses of who He was in the law and prophets. The moral law as given through Moses reflected the heart and character of God. God's works of mercy and declarations of His character in the Old Testament narratives revealed He was just, holy, merciful, gracious, and a loving Father.

Jesus is the full revelation of God's character. In Him, "the whole fullness of deity" dwelled bodily (Colossians 2:9). John expands and says, "And the Word became flesh and dwelt among us, and we have seen his glory, glory as of the only Son from the Father, full of grace and truth... for the law was given through Moses; grace and truth came through Jesus Christ" (John 1:14-16).

Jesus is the fulfillment of the Messiah prophesied about in the Old Testament. He confirmed this several times in the gospels. In Luke 4:18-21 He says of Isaiah 61, "Today this scripture is fulfilled in your hearing." And after His resurrection, "beginning with Moses and all the prophets, he (Jesus) interpreted to them in all the Scriptures the things concerning himself" (Luke 24:27).

Jesus fulfilled the moral law by perfectly obeying the law and fulfilling all righteousness (Matthew 3:15). He also came to explain the full and true meaning of the law, which we will see in verses 21-48.

Jesus filled and completed the ceremonial law and sacrificial system, in that the goal of the sacrificial system was to point to Christ (Hebrews 9).

Jesus expressed that all the scripture would be fulfilled. Not even an "iota or dot," the smallest part of the law, would pass away until it is accomplished. In saying this, "Jesus affirms the reliability and truthfulness of the scriptures with the strongest possible language" (Akin, 30). Jesus declared that the word of God was perfect and without error.

Verses 19-20

The Pharisees and scribes had "relaxed" the commandments. They had reduced them to a list of outward behaviors to impress others and check off items on a checklist. Jesus clarified that the law was indeed meant to be kept, but it was to be kept in a way that was from the heart- out of love for God and neighbor. He clarified that the righteousness God requires to "enter the kingdom of heaven" involves more than just an outward checklist of the Pharisees or the vast knowledge of the scribes. It is the righteousness that comes with a new heart that is obtained by acknowledging "poverty in spirit" and one's need for the mercy and grace of God.

Application & Reflection

1. How does knowing that Jesus fulfills the Old Testament change the way we read it?

2. How does Jesus' view of scripture inform our confidence in scripture?

3. Read **Jeremiah 31:33** and **Ezekiel 36:26-28**. These describe the "new heart" righteousness the prophets foresaw and that we experience with new-birth in Christ. Based on these prophesies and Matthew 5:17-20, what is the relationship with this righteousness and the law?

Jeremiah 31:33

33 For this is the covenant that I will make with the house of Israel after those days, declares the Lord: I will put my law within them, and I will write it on their hearts. And I will be their God, and they shall be my people.

Ezekiel 36:26-28

26 And I will give you a new heart, and a new spirit I will put within you. And I will remove the heart of stone from your flesh and give you a heart of flesh. 27 And I will put my Spirit within you and cause you to walk in my statutes and be careful to obey my rules. 28 You shall dwell in the land that I gave to your fathers, and you shall be my people, and I will be your God.

4. Read **2 Corinthians 5:21** and **1 John 1:7-10**. How are we to go about obtaining this "surpassing righteousness?"

2 Corinthians 5:21

[21] For our sake he made him to be sin who knew no sin, so that in him we might become the righteousness of God.

1 John 1:7-10

[7] But if we walk in the light, as he is in the light, we have fellowship with one another, and the blood of Jesus his Son cleanses us from all sin. [8] If we say we have no sin, we deceive ourselves, and the truth is not in us. [9] If we confess our sins, he is faithful and just to forgive us our sins and to cleanse us from all unrighteousness. [10] If we say we have not sinned, we make him a liar, and his word is not in us.

Lesson 6
A Righteousness from the Heart
Matthew 5:21–32 (Part 1)

Observation & Interpretation

Read Matthew 5:21-32 and consider the following questions.

[21] "You have heard that it was said to those of old, 'You shall not murder; and whoever murders will be liable to judgment.' [22] But I say to you that everyone who is angry with his brother will be liable to judgment; whoever insults his brother will be liable to the council; and whoever says, 'You fool!' will be liable to the hell[e] of fire. [23] So if you are offering your gift at the altar and there remember that your brother has something against you, [24] leave your gift there before the altar and go. First be reconciled to your brother, and then come and offer your gift. [25] Come to terms quickly with your accuser while you are going with him to court, lest your accuser hand you over to the judge, and the judge to the guard, and you be put in prison. [26] Truly, I say to you, you will never get out until you have paid the last penny.[f]

[27] "You have heard that it was said, 'You shall not commit adultery.'[28] But I say to you that everyone who looks at a woman with lustful intent has already committed adultery with her in his heart. [29] If your right eye causes you to sin, tear it out and throw it away. For it is better that you lose one of your members than that your whole body be thrown into hell. [30] And if your right hand causes you to sin, cut it off and throw it away. For it is better that you lose one of your members than that your whole body go into hell.

[31] "It was also said, 'Whoever divorces his wife, let him give her a certificate of divorce.' [32] But I say to you that everyone who divorces his wife, except on the ground of sexual immorality, makes

her commit adultery, and whoever marries a divorced woman commits adultery.

1. Matthew 5:17-20 is an introduction to 21-48. How does Jesus' view of the law in 17-20 help us understand His explanation in verses 21-48?

2. In the chart below, list the differences between what they "have heard it said" about obedience by the Pharisees and what Jesus teaches about obedience.

"You have heard it said…."	Jesus said:
Murder:	
Adultery:	
Divorce:	

3. Sum up Jesus' clarification on the law in your own words.

4. **Matthew 19:3-9** gives us another situation where Jesus taught about divorce. Read this passage and consider the following questions.

[3] And Pharisees came up to him and tested him by asking, "Is it lawful to divorce one's wife for any cause?" [4] He answered, "Have you not read that he who created them from the beginning made them male and female,
[5] and said, 'Therefore a man shall leave his father and his mother and hold fast to his wife, and the two shall become one flesh'?
[6] So they are no longer two but one flesh. What therefore God has joined together, let not man separate." [7] They said to him, "Why then did Moses command one to give a certificate of divorce and to send her away?" [8] He said to them, "Because of your hardness of heart Moses allowed you to divorce your wives, but from the beginning it was not so. [9] And I say to you: whoever divorces his wife, except for sexual immorality, and marries another, commits adultery."

What insight does this context give you when thinking about Jesus' clarification of the law on divorce?

How does this help you understand how the Pharisees and scribes changed/omitted these commands?

Commentary

The Pharisees and scribes had either taught a "bare minimum" approach to obedience to the law, or they had twisted the law altogether. In Matthew 5:21-48, Jesus addressed common deceptive "relaxations" of the law when He said repeatedly, "You have heard it said..." He followed these by explaining: 1. The true interpretation of the law as it reflects the heart of God and 2. The righteousness required for the Kingdom of heaven that "exceeds that of the scribes and Pharisees" (Matthew 5:20). Verses 21-48 are often called "the antitheses."

As we study Jesus' explanation of the law in the rest of chapter 5, it might feel crushing to us. It may feel tempting for us too, to "relax" these commands. Just like the Pharisees and scribes, we may find the "yoke" of the law burdensome and difficult to carry.

Jesus said, "Come to me, all who labor and are heavy laden, and I will give you rest. Take my yoke upon you, and learn from me, for I am gentle and lowly in heart, and you will find rest for your souls. For my yoke is easy and my burden is light" (Matthew 11:28-30). Jesus has hopeful words to those who find the requirements of the law burdensome. He instructs them to deal with this weight, not by "relaxing" the commandments, but by coming to Him. He said, "my yoke is easy and my burden is light." As we consider Matthew 5:21-48, we will reflect on how a Christian can obey God's law while resting in the One who fulfilled the law (Matthew 5:17). We will pursue the "surpassing righteousness" required of us by hoping in the righteousness and the "gentle and lowly" heart of Christ.

By His spirit and His example, we pursue obedience to these commands. Not out of rote routine or reluctant compulsion, but that we may live in the way we were created to: reflecting our Father's character, set apart as His family, and rejoicing in His love and glory.

Verses 21-22

Jesus started His explanations by expounding on the command "You shall not murder..." (Exodus 20:13 and Deuteronomy 5:17). The teaching of the day limited the application of this to the actual act of murder. However, Jesus explained that murder carried out in action, murder in our hearts, and murder through our words are all subject to judgment and "the hell of fire." This is shocking language to us, and it would have been shocking for Jesus' original audience as well. With this statement He clarified the seriousness of sin and the importance of a pure heart (Matthew 5:6). When we are adopted into God's kingdom, "do not murder" means do not murder your brother or sister in your heart.

Verses 23-26

What does this mean practically? Jesus gave two examples: one of anger towards a brother or sister and one with an "accuser." The first is of someone "offering their gift at the altar" when they remember their brother or sister has something against them. This implies, not a slight misunderstanding or hint of aggravation, but a real grievance or conflict between brothers. He said, "first be reconciled to your brother, and then come and offer your gift." God cares not just about our coming to Him in religious routines and outward obedience ("at the altar"). He is primarily concerned about our heart. James expands on this in his letter when he talks about the danger of our words, "With it [the tongue] we bless our Lord and Father, and with it we curse people who are made in the likeness of God.
From the same mouth come blessing and cursing. My brothers, these things not ought to be so" (James 3:9-10). We are to repent and restore relationships with others before we "come and offer our gift" or serve God in formal ministry. Just like a parent who is not pleased with outward obedience when their child refuses to resolve open conflict with their sibling, God our Father prioritizes reconciled relationships between brothers and sisters.

The next application involves an "accuser" or someone who is taking you to court. Jesus said that things should be settled quickly. Similarly, Paul wrote to the Romans, "If possible, so far as it depends on you, live peaceably with all" (Romans 12:18). Overall, these words challenge us to deal with the thoughts in our heart right away, before more damage is caused; whether this danger be anger, slander, murder, or "paying of the last penny."

Verses 27-30

Next, Jesus addressed adultery. A married person is not to have a sexual relationship with anyone other than his or her spouse. And Jesus clarified that the command "You shall not commit adultery" (Exodus 20:14, Deuteronomy 5:18) has deeper, fuller intentions. He explained that this command included the physical act of adultery, and looking at another with "lustful intent" in the heart.
Gazing or imagining in sexual excitement over someone you are not married with is adultery. Again, God is after our hearts. His intention is that the children of God would not only refrain from outward sexual sin, but that we would love God and others in a way that refuses to use others for our own selfish pleasure. Jesus loves us and is for our good; therefore, we are to love others and be for their good. We are not to use others for selfish gain. As believers love God with their hearts, they will resolve to love, value, and esteem those made in God's image, not objectify them.

In 29-30, Jesus gets practical in telling them how to avoid adultery. In doing so, He gives insight into how all our sin should be viewed and dealt with. "If your right eye causes you to sin... tear it out and throw it away." These illustrations are hyperbole in order to express the severity and danger of sin. The applications vary, but the principle is: sin is serious and dangerous, and drastic measures must be taken to avoid it.

Practical measures are necessary and helpful in pursuing pure thoughts. However, as Jesus has already taught, purity is primarily an issue of the heart. We can obey God's design for purity in the deep way He intends when He gives us a new heart by His Holy spirit. As we walk in repentance and behold the One who loves perfectly, purely, and selflessly, He will "wash us whiter than snow" and "create in us a clean heart" (Psalm 51:7,10). Our eyes and bodies will surely follow.

Verses 31-32

As Jesus teaches, God's heart and holiness continue to be revealed. In verses 31-32 we see God's high, holy view of marriage. God's design is that marriages are to endure for a lifetime. More insight is provided in Matthew 19:3-9 when Jesus is asked by the Pharisees, "Is it lawful to divorce one's wife for any cause?"
Jesus referred to creation, and said, "'Therefore a man shall leave his father and mother and hold fast to his wife, and the two shall become one flesh?' So they are no longer two but one flesh. What therefore God has joined together, let not man separate."
Ephesians 5 clarifies that the marriage relationship is designed to be a picture of Christ's forever enduring relationship with His church. It is with this view of marriage in mind that Jesus spoke to the practice of divorce.

In Jesus' day, there were two schools of thought on the teaching of divorce in Deuteronomy 24:1-4. Daniel Akin explains, "The school of Shammai taught that sexual sin was the only permissible reason to end a marriage by divorce. The school of Hillel argued that anything a wife did that displeased her husband provided valid grounds for divorce" (Akin, 58). The more popular teaching, the school of Hillel, allowed one to divorce their spouse for any reason. Both in Matthew 5 and 19, Jesus dismissed the idea that a divorce is lawful "for any cause."

"You have heard it said, if anyone divorces his wife, let him give her a certificate of divorce. But I say to you, anyone who divorces his wife, except on the grounds of sexual immorality, makes her commit adultery, and anyone who marries a divorced woman commits adultery." Today, this principle applies to both spouses, but since a man divorcing his wife was the more common practice of Jesus' day, Jesus addressed this from the perspective of a man initiating divorce.

He included the exception that it is permissible to divorce when one's spouse has been sexually immoral. Though even in the case of sexual immorality, divorce is never commanded or encouraged. God hates divorce (Malachi 2:16) and desires healing and reconciliation in marriage.

Further, He speaks into a situation where a wife would remarry. This would be expected in this culture/time due to the need for a woman to seek financial support through marriage, but again, this principle regarding remarriage applies to a man or a woman. There is a profound mystery about marriage in that two become one flesh (Ephesians 5:31-32). God's ideal and design for marriage is permanent and lifelong—therefore, to divorce one's spouse on unbiblical grounds and remarry is to commit adultery.

We should not conclude that Jesus' intention here was to give an exhaustive teaching on the practical implications of marriage and divorce. Practical application to these teachings and decisions about remarriage after divorce go beyond what we are able to cover in this study. These decisions should be made alongside pastors and elders in the church after honest conversation and prayer. Additional passages to consult on these issues include: 1 Corinthians 7, Ephesians 5:22-32, Deuteronomy 24:1-4, Matthew 19:3-9, and Malachi 2:13-16.

As we receive Jesus' words toward the painful reality of divorce, we must be mindful of the speaker and His experience. Jesus knows what it is like to be abandoned and betrayed by those He loved. He was without fault, but "he was despised and rejected by men... pierced for our transgressions and crushed for our iniquities" (Isaiah 53:3,5). And because of His rejection, when we confess our sins, He is faithful and just to forgive us our sins and remove them as far as the east is from the west (I John 1:9, Psalm 103:12). He is a comforter to those who mourn (Matthew 5:4) and our great sympathizer who gives grace in the time of need (Hebrews 4:14-16). As for the pain caused by abandonment, divorce, adultery, or immorality, God is a healer; and "he will bind up the broken-hearted" (Isaiah 61:1).

As the family of God, we have received new hearts and the Holy Spirit through the gospel. By the Spirit, we are able to be faithful to our spouses in ways that the rest of the world can't. When we are "poor in spirit" and understand our great need for mercy, we can extend that mercy to our spouse; we do not cast them off for "any cause." As we seek this righteousness in marriage that "exceeds the scribes and pharisees" (Matthew 5:20), we can only hope in the righteousness and faithfulness of Christ. We can look with hope and comfort to the One who through rejection and abandonment, faithfully endured the cross and gave Himself up for His bride.

Application & Reflection

1. What does Jesus' interpretation of the law tell us about the heart of God?

2. In this study, we are looking at the Sermon on the Mount in light of our adoption into God's family. If we carry out Jesus' calling to obedience in 21-32, how might it help us to know and love God the Father more?

How might it cause us to reflect our Father more?

3. What about Jesus' words are challenging to you? What is comforting to you?

4. How does the fact that Jesus fulfills the law inform the way we apply these verses?

Lesson 7
A Righteousness from the Heart
Matthew 5:33–48 (Part 2)

Observation & Interpretation

Read Matthew 5:33–48 and consider the following questions.

[33] "Again you have heard that it was said to those of old, 'You shall not swear falsely, but shall perform to the Lord what you have sworn.'[34] But I say to you, Do not take an oath at all, either by heaven, for it is the throne of God, [35] or by the earth, for it is his footstool, or by Jerusalem, for it is the city of the great King. [36] And do not take an oath by your head, for you cannot make one hair white or black. [37] Let what you say be simply 'Yes' or 'No'; anything more than this comes from evil.

[38] "You have heard that it was said, 'An eye for an eye and a tooth for a tooth.' [39] But I say to you, do not resist the one who is evil. But if anyone slaps you on the right cheek, turn to him the other also.[40] And if anyone would sue you and take your tunic, let him have your cloak as well. [41] And if anyone forces you to go one mile, go with him two miles. [42] Give to the one who begs from you, and do not refuse the one who would borrow from you.

[43] "You have heard that it was said, 'You shall love your neighbor and hate your enemy.' [44] But I say to you, love your enemies and pray for those who persecute you, [45] so that you may be sons of your Father who is in heaven. For he makes his sun rise on the evil and on the good, and sends rain on the just and on the unjust. [46] For if you love those who love you, what reward do you have? Do not even the tax collectors do the same? [47] And if you greet only your brothers, what more are you doing than others? Do not even the Gentiles do the same? [48] You therefore must be perfect, as your heavenly Father is perfect.

1. In the chart below, list the differences between what they "have heard it said" about obedience by the Pharisees and what Jesus teaches about obedience.

	"You have heard it said…"	Jesus said…
Oaths		
Personal justice		
Relating to enemies		

2. Read **Matthew 23:16-22** (on oaths) and **Leviticus 19:17-18** (on relating to neighbors and enemies) and consider the following questions.

[16] "Woe to you, blind guides, who say, 'If anyone swears by the temple, it is nothing, but if anyone swears by the gold of the temple, he is bound by his oath.' [17] You blind fools! For which is greater, the gold or the temple that has made the gold sacred? [18] And you say, 'If anyone swears by the altar, it is nothing, but if anyone swears by the gift that is on the altar, he is bound by his oath.'

19 You blind men! For which is greater, the gift or the altar that makes the gift sacred? **20** So whoever swears by the altar swears by it and by everything on it.**21** And whoever swears by the temple swears by it and by him who dwells in it. **22** And whoever swears by heaven swears by the throne of God and by him who sits upon it.

17 "You shall not hate your brother in your heart, but you shall reason frankly with your neighbor, lest you incur sin because of him. **18** You shall not take vengeance or bear a grudge against the sons of your own people, but you shall love your neighbor as yourself: I am the Lord.

What insight do these verses give you as you think about Jesus' clarification of the law?

3. How had the Pharisees and scribes changed/omitted these commands?

Commentary

Verses 33-37

Next, Jesus speaks into our verbal commitments before God and others. He quoted Numbers 30:2 and said, "you have heard it said, 'you shall not swear falsely but shall perform to the Lord what you have sworn.'" We see in Matthew 23:16-22 that the Pharisees had created a system of loopholes and had assisted in insincerity with words. They taught that words before God were important, and words in our human relationships were less important. Jesus corrected this and taught that our words before God and others are all to be equally sincere and honest.

He calls us to another approach in verse 34, "Do not take an oath at all.." Though oaths themselves were not bad (Jesus himself often said "truly I say to you" on important matters and God made oaths as well in Genesis 9:9-11 and Genesis 22:17), Jesus was against the tendency to only be sincere when certain "oath" language was used.

Jesus instructed them not take an oath by heaven, earth, Jerusalem, or their own head. All of these things are under God's control, not man's. When we fear God and understand our limited capacity, our words are humble.
Instead, we are to simply say, "yes or no," and our "yeses" and "nos" should be trustworthy. Every part of our speech should be true and full of integrity—therefore, we should not have to use special emphasis of oaths or swearing to convince people we are telling the truth. As God's children, our language before our Father and, also, before those made in His image, should be truthful and sincere.

Verses 38-42

Next Jesus spoke into how a disciple should think of retaliation and personal justice. "You have heard that it was said, 'An eye for an eye and a tooth for a tooth.'" This passage is from Exodus 21:24 and in the context it is a principle for how to determine consequences in the courtroom. It instructed judges to give a punishment equal to the crime committed. Jesus did not have a problem with the intended, courtroom use of this principle.

But in verses 39-42, He corrected what seems to be a practice of applying "eye for eye" in personal relationships and circumstances. He laid down a new principle, "Do not resist the one who is evil." Even when we are mistreated, we are not to "resist" or retaliate. Paul elaborates in Romans 12:17-21 when he instructs us not to avenge ourselves, but to bless and serve our enemies when they are in need.

Jesus used four examples that related to the culture. Verse 39 tells us to "turn the other cheek" and not to retaliate against an insulting "slap," but be willing to endure further insult (39). In a legal dispute, a tunic (shirt) was often used for bartering and making payments (Akin, 39). Jesus instructed that they should not just give the required payment of the tunic but also be willing to offer their coat, the more valuable garment. Next, Israel was under the occupation of Rome, and Roman soldiers could often force the Israelites to serve them. One example is in Mark 15:21 when Simon of Cyrene was forced by Roman soldiers to carry the cross of Jesus. Jesus challenged them, "when someone forces you to go one mile, go with them two miles" (40). Lastly, Jesus told His disciples to be ready and willing to assist those in need (42).

John Stott addresses hesitation we may have: are these examples to be taken literally? He suggests perhaps there will be times we do need to obey these verses literally (Jesus certainly did). But he helpfully points out that since Jesus' teaching is given to us in illustrations rather than detailed regulations, we do not need to "take the four little cameos with wooden, unimaginative literalism." But Jesus' illustrations are certainly explaining an important principle. Stott continues, "That principle is love, the selfless love of a person who, when injured, refuses to satisfy himself by taking revenge, but studies instead the highest welfare of the other person and of society, and determines his actions accordingly.
He will certainly never hit back, returning evil for evil, for he has been entirely freed from personal animosity. Instead, he seeks to return good from evil. So he is willing to give to the uttermost—his body, his clothing, his service, his money—in so far as these gifts are required by love" (107).

As always, Jesus' humble heart and life of service is the best commentary on His teaching. Peter describes Jesus' response to suffering, including being slapped by Roman soldiers (Matthew 26:67-68). "When he was reviled, he did not revile in return; when he suffered, he did not threaten, but continued entrusting himself to him who judges justly" (1 Peter 2:23). We were in need, so Jesus, in merciful generosity towards us, "Though he was rich... for your sake he became poor, so that you by his poverty might become rich" (2 Corinthians 8:9). When we inevitably experience pain and then desire for retaliation, we can lift our gaze to Jesus. He was despised and rejected but responded with meekness, humble service, and generosity — all while entrusting Himself to His Father.

Verses 43-48

The last section starts with, "You have heard that it was said, love your neighbor and hate your enemies." Apparently, this had been the Pharisees' and scribes' interpretation of Leviticus 19:18, "Love your neighbor as yourself." But there are some obvious problems. The Pharisees and scribes had taken off the phrase, "as yourself" and added, "and hate your enemies." The phrase "hate your enemies" is nowhere in the Old Testament. This addition encouraged behavior and attitudes that were grossly far from the calling of Christ.

Jesus gives the correct way we are to view others, "But I say to you, love your enemies and pray for those who persecute you" (44). This implies active, ongoing service and love toward "enemies." So, really this means that we are not to view them as enemies at all but as neighbors. He also tells us to pray for them, implying on-going loving action, affection that has their best interest in mind, and a posture of humility before God.

Why? "So that you may be sons of your Father who is in heaven." We are to take on the likeness of our Father. God does not make the sun rise on only the good or send rain on only the just (45). God is merciful to all.

Outside of the family of God, people love those who love them. That's a natural thing to do. We won't receive a heavenly reward for that (46). People of all backgrounds can greet the ones they know well, that's easy. Everyone can do that. Jesus challenged His disciples, "what more are you doing than others?" (47). It is not enough for the children of God to be like everyone else. Because, if we have been kindly and graciously welcomed by God, we can be kind and gracious to all. If we have believed and experienced that "while we were still enemies we were reconciled to God by the death of his son" (Romans 5:10), we, too, can love our enemies. If our brother is Christ, who went before us and prayed for His "enemies" as they mocked Him, saying, "Father, forgive them, because they do not know what they are doing" (Luke 23:34), then we, like Jesus, can pray for those who persecute us. We can take on His likeness, and be "perfect as He is perfect" (48).

Application & Reflection

1. How do Jesus' words confront you?

2. What does Jesus' interpretation of the law tell us about the heart of God?

3. If we carry out Jesus' calling to obedience in 33-48, how might it help us to know and love God the Father more? How might it cause us to reflect our Father more?

4. "**Come to me, all who labor and are heavy laden, and I will give you rest. Take my yoke upon you, and learn from me, for I am gentle and lowly in heart, and you will find rest for your souls.**" **Matthew 11:28-29**

Is there a call to obedience in Matthew 5:21-48 that feels heavy and difficult?

How can Jesus' interpretation and heart encourage you in repentance and obedience?

4. Read **1 Peter 2:21-25** and consider the following questions.

[21] For to this you have been called, because Christ also suffered for you, leaving you an example, so that you might follow in his steps. [22] He committed no sin, neither was deceit found in his mouth. [23] When he was reviled, he did not revile in return; when he

suffered, he did not threaten, but continued entrusting himself to him who judges justly. [24] He himself bore our sins in his body on the tree, that we might die to sin and live to righteousness.
By his wounds you have been healed. [25] For you were straying like sheep, but have now returned to the Shepherd and Overseer of your souls.

How did Jesus live out the righteousness in Matthew 5:21-48?

How does Jesus' example encourage you as you seek to imitate Him and "be perfect as your Father is perfect?" (48)

5. God our Father calls His children to look different from the rest of the world (Matthew 5:44-48). How might this lead you to pray?

Lesson 8
The Family of God and Spiritual Disciplines
Matthew 6:1–6, 16–18

Observation & Interpretation

Read Matthew 6:1–6, 16–18 and consider the following questions.

[1]"Beware of practicing your righteousness before other people in order to be seen by them, for then you will have no reward from your Father who is in heaven.

[2] "Thus, when you give to the needy, sound no trumpet before you, as the hypocrites do in the synagogues and in the streets, that they may be praised by others. Truly, I say to you, they have received their reward. [3] But when you give to the needy, do not let your left hand know what your right hand is doing, [4] so that your giving may be in secret. And your Father who sees in secret will reward you.

[5] "And when you pray, you must not be like the hypocrites. For they love to stand and pray in the synagogues and at the street corners, that they may be seen by others. Truly, I say to you, they have received their reward. [6] But when you pray, go into your room and shut the door and pray to your Father who is in secret. And your Father who sees in secret will reward you.

[16] "And when you fast, do not look gloomy like the hypocrites, for they disfigure their faces that their fasting may be seen by others. Truly, I say to you, they have received their reward. [17] But when you fast, anoint your head and wash your face, [18] that your fasting may not be seen by others but by your Father who is in secret. And your Father who sees in secret will reward you.

1. What is the warning Jesus gave in Matthew 6:1-2?

2. What do you think is the difference between letting "your light shine before others" (Matthew 5:16) and "practicing your righteousness in order to be seen by others?" (Matthew 6:1)

3. Describe the application of the warning given regarding:

      Giving:

      Prayer:

      Fasting:

4. In Jesus' life, how did He exemplify living a life for His Father's reward?

Commentary

As we continue to study how we should live as disciples of Christ, Jesus elaborates on two new categories in Chapter 6: our spiritual disciplines and our treasures. As for our spiritual disciplines, how does knowing that we are loved sons and daughters inform things like giving, prayer, and fasting?

Verse 1

Jesus warned that we are to "beware" of practicing our righteousness before others in order to be seen by them. The Message paraphrases this verse, "Be especially careful when you are trying to be good so that you don't make a performance out of it. It might be good theater, but the God who made you won't be applauding" (MSG). Though our righteousness *is* to be seen, the purpose of it being seen is so that God our Father will be glorified (Matthew 5:16). Jesus warned about the danger of "practicing righteousness" with the prideful motivation of seeking others' approval. Why? "For then you will receive no reward from your Father who is in heaven." As God's true Son, Jesus knew of the intimate fellowship that could be ours if our righteousness was done for God's glory, "in secret." John Stott explains, "We have to be so conscious of God that we cease to be self-conscious" (Stott, 140). As Jesus already mentioned in Matthew 5:6, those with a pure heart, who give, pray, and fast while seeking God alone; they are the ones that "see" God their Father.

Verses 2-4

His first example in how to practice righteousness is of giving to the needy. Some translations say, "when you give alms." This example refers to giving to people who would sit outside the temple and ask for money (See Acts 3:1-10). It was a practical way of giving in Jesus' time.

Today, the principles here can apply to our giving to those in need.

The word "hypocrite" was originally used to refer to an actor who performed on stage. Here Jesus used it to describe someone who acts one way on the outside and is completely different on the inside. Unlike the hypocrites, we are not to draw attention to ourselves when we give; we are not actors on a stage. We are not even to "let [our] left hand know what [our] right hand is doing." That is, we are not even to acknowledge our giving to ourselves or congratulate ourselves. We are to give "in secret" or only for the audience of our Heavenly Father.

Underneath the act of giving "to be seen by others" lies a belief that our resources are our own, obtained by our own efforts, and ours to control and give as we choose. But the belief and trust in God as our generous Father leads us to see ourselves as stewards. The only resources we have are those which He gives by His grace.

Our money and possessions are on loan to us from our Father; therefore, to give to those in need is stewarding our possessions in a way that worships and honors Him. As we give, we experience the reward of gratitude for what God has given us. We experience reward in our joy as we help those that God loves. Our giving is an offering of what God has given us back to God Himself. "...A fragrant offering, a sacrifice acceptable and pleasing to God" (Philippians 4:18).

Verses 5-6

Similarly, our prayer is not a performance. Jesus said of the hypocrites who "stand in the synagogues and the street corners so they may be praised by others…" – the reward they seek is others' approval, and so they have received their reward. There is no need to pray longer or use different words in public prayer than when we pray on our own. Prayer in public is not wrong, but praying primarily "before others in order to be seen by them" is a tragic forfeiting of the intimacy with God available to us in Christ. Prayer should reflect a genuine conversation with our Father.

Jesus encourages us to guard and treasure the times we "go into [our] room and shut the door, and pray to [our] Father who is in secret." We see in Romans 8:15-16 that it is when our hearts cry "Abba Father" that God's spirit testifies with our spirit that we are His children. There is no greater peace and satisfaction than this. Jesus Himself often withdrew away to pray alone or "in secret," and everything He did was to please His Heavenly Father (John 8:29). We should follow His example in seeking the reward of God's presence and fellowship in prayer.

Verses 16-18

The same principles apply to fasting. The "hypocrites" would try to show their discomfort in fasting by disfiguring their faces; their aim was to draw attention to themselves and receive pity from others. But Jesus encouraged His disciples to seek a greater reward. To "anoint your head and wash your face" was a habit of normal selfcare in this time. Jesus was saying, do what you would normally do. When we fast, we are to look normal. There is no need to try to be seen by others. Our pleas when we fast are for our Father to hear and see; He will see us and reward us.

Application & Reflection

1. Do you practice spiritual disciplines like prayer, giving, and fasting in public differently than you do in private? If so, does your heart reflect a desire to "be seen by others"?

2. How does your adoption into God's family inform the way you view spiritual disciplines?

3. When have you received the Father's reward in your giving, prayer, and/or fasting?

4. What would your spiritual disciplines look like if they were done solely "for your Father who is in secret"?

What changes will you make to your habits so that you can receive the reward only our Father can give?

Lesson 9
A Family Prayer
Matthew 6:7–15

Observation & Interpretation

Read Matthew 6:7–15 and consider the following questions.

[7] "And when you pray, do not heap up empty phrases as the Gentiles do, for they think that they will be heard for their many words. [8] Do not be like them, for your Father knows what you need before you ask him. [9] Pray then like this:

"Our Father in heaven,
hallowed be your name.
[10] Your kingdom come,
your will be done,
    on earth as it is in heaven.
[11] Give us this day our daily bread,
[12] and forgive us our debts,
    as we also have forgiven our debtors.
[13] And lead us not into temptation,
    but deliver us from evil.

[14] For if you forgive others their trespasses, your heavenly Father will also forgive you, [15] but if you do not forgive others their trespasses, neither will your Father forgive your trespasses.

1. According to verses 7 and 8, what are we NOT to do when we pray?

2. From verses 7 and 8, what is the difference between the way the "gods" of the Gentiles were approached and way we approach our Heavenly Father?

3. Verses 9 and 10 focus on Who we are praying to. What do you learn about God from verses 9 and 10?

4. Verses 11-13 lead us to express our own physical and spiritual needs. What does Jesus tell us to ask for?

Commentary

Verses 7 and 8

Previously, Jesus warned of the danger of praying like the hypocrites, and in verses 7 and 8 He warned not to pray like the Gentiles. The Gentiles did not acknowledge the God of Israel. They believed that with their prayers, their gods could be manipulated. The Gentiles would "heap up empty phrases" so they could be heard.

Jesus explained that our God is different. There is no formula or set of phrases we need to use to be assured of His listening, and in His infinite wisdom, He can't be manipulated. Instead, He has the knowledge and care of a good Father who loves us and, "knows what we need before we ask." God hears us and is ready to answer, and we don't have to convince Him to listen with special phrases. J.I. Packer explains, "Jesus could say to his Father, 'You always hear me' (John 11:42), and he wants his disciples to know that, as God's adopted children, the same is true of them" (212). We are to pray with a posture of childlike trust to our Father. What does this look like? Jesus gave us an outline. We are to "pray then like this..."

Verse 9

"Our Father who is in heaven." This is a family prayer. We are praying to our Father in heaven—the one who adopted us as sons and daughters through Jesus Christ (Galatians 4:5-6). We are to pray, "Hallowed be your name..." The CSB translates this, "Your name be honored as Holy." As children in His family that know His worthiness and goodness, we pray and desire that His "name," the essence and identity of His character, would be honored; that He would be glorified through our lives (Matthew 5:16). As our hearts focus fully on His Fatherly care and holy name, this then guides the rest of our requests.

Verse 10

"Your Kingdom come, your will be done, on earth as it is in heaven." When we love our Father and desire His glory, we long for His Kingdom to come. John Stott explains, "To pray that his kingdom may 'come' is to pray both that it may grow, as through the church's witness people submit to Jesus, and that soon it will be consummated when Jesus returns in glory to take his power and reign" (147). We are given many glimpses of God's kingdom in heaven throughout the Old and New Testament.

The promise of God's eternal Kingdom leads us to yearn, and therefore pray, for His Kingdom come. In order for this to happen, we pray, "your will be done." God's will is perfect and is always for His glory (Romans 8:28). When God is glorified in His will, it is the means He uses to "make all things new" (Revelation 21:5) and bring His Kingdom here on earth "as it is in heaven..."

As we consider the example of Jesus praying, "not as I will but as you will" before He went to the cross (Matthew 26:39) we recognize, as Daniel Akin explains, "The will of God is not always easy, and it is not always safe. But as Paul teaches in Romans 12:2, it is always 'good, pleasing and perfect'" (95). We pray for His Kingdom in our world, our own lives, our relationships, and our hearts. In doing so, this may mean humble, sacrificial obedience; enduring persecution for the name of Jesus; laying down our desires and dreams; loving our enemies; forgiving deep hurts; reconciling and restoring relationships; denying ourselves, taking up our crosses, and following Jesus (Luke 9:23). We pray for God's will, not ours; God's glory, not ours; God's kingdom, not ours. And just like God's perfect will in the life of Jesus, His perfect will in our lives is what He is using to redeem and "make all things new" for His glory, our good, and His Kingdom come.

Verse 11

"Give us this day our daily bread..." With our eternal home in mind, we ask God to sustain us with daily provision for our home on this earth. This includes physical and spiritual provision.

Just as God provided manna in the wilderness every day until the Israelites ate the fruit of the promised land (Joshua 5:12), God will provide us with our daily bread until He brings us home to heaven. And just like the Israelites were fully and completely dependent on God for their daily bread; we, whether we realize it or not, are fully dependent on God's grace and provision for our daily bread. Many of us take things like meals for granted, but everything we have is a gift from our gracious Father; we should ask and trust Him accordingly.

God also provides for our spiritual needs. As Jesus has already mentioned, when we hunger and thirst for righteousness, we will be satisfied (Matthew 5:6). Jesus is the bread of life. He sustains us by His word, manna that fills us full (John 6:32-35).

Verse 12

Included in our daily needs is our need for forgiveness, so we pray, "Forgive us our debts." Our forgiveness and right standing before God is essential for our soul, like bread for the body. If we belong to God, there is "no condemnation for those in Christ Jesus" (Romans 8:1). But we must confess our sin to make things right with our Father. God forgives our debt, "as we forgive our debtors." John Stott explains, "This certainly does not mean that our forgiveness of others earns us the right to be forgiven. It is rather that God forgives only the penitent and one of the chief evidences of true penitence is a forgiving spirit" (149).

Receiving forgiveness from God sets in motion a cycle of mercy, humility, and forgiveness for our own sins and others' sins against us. This part of the prayer asks for mercy and forgiveness for our sins, and that our awareness of mercy would lead to our forgiveness of others' sins against us.

Verse 13

Lastly, we are to pray, "Lead us not into temptation, but deliver us from evil." When we receive forgiveness for our debts, we pray earnestly that we would not fall into temptation to sin again. God Himself never tempts us, but we are drawn to evil by our own hearts (James 1:13-14). We need God's help, a way to endure under temptation (1 Corinthians 10:13). Jesus directs us to pray so that we might not enter temptation, just as He instructed His disciples in the garden to "watch and pray that they might not fall into temptation" (Luke 22:40). God will provide this help when we ask. Through Christ in us and in His Church, He will provide a way out of temptation and deliver us from evil.

Verses 14 and 15

Here Jesus expanded on verse 12. God's forgiveness of us is to translate into our forgiveness of others. When we have experienced God's forgiveness and have a sense of our great need for mercy, we will extend mercy to others. As Ephesians 4:32 says, "Forgive others as God in Christ has forgiven you."

Application & Reflection

Use this time to pray or journal through this prayer now, according to your own thoughts, needs, and circumstances.

"Our Father in heaven,
hallowed be your name.
Your kingdom come,
your will be done,
on earth as it is in heaven.
Give us this day our daily bread,
and forgive us our debts,
as we also have forgiven our debtors.
And lead us not into temptation,
but deliver us from evil."

Lesson 10
The Treasure of the Family of God
Matthew 6:19–24

Observation & Interpretation

Read Matthew 6:19–24 and consider the following questions.

[19] "Do not lay up for yourselves treasures on earth, where moth and rust destroy and where thieves break in and steal, [20] but lay up for yourselves treasures in heaven, where neither moth nor rust destroys and where thieves do not break in and steal. [21] For where your treasure is, there your heart will be also.

[22] "The eye is the lamp of the body. So, if your eye is healthy, your whole body will be full of light, [23] but if your eye is bad, your whole body will be full of darkness. If then the light in you is darkness, how great is the darkness!

[24] "No one can serve two masters, for either he will hate the one and love the other, or he will be devoted to the one and despise the other. You cannot serve God and money.

1. Considering the other parts of the sermon we have studied, what do you think Jesus meant when He said, "treasure in heaven"?

2. What is the difference between treasure on earth and treasure in heaven?

What happens to our hearts when we "store up" treasure on earth?

3. Our heart's treasure (19-21) often leads to our vision or purpose (22-23). How does what we treasure affect our spiritual "vision" of our life?

4. Read **James 4:4** and **Romans 6:16**. Why is it impossible to "serve two masters"? (24)

⁴ You adulterous people! Do you not know that friendship with the world is enmity with God? Therefore whoever wishes to be a friend of the world makes himself an enemy of God.

¹⁶ Do you not know that if you present yourselves to anyone as obedient slaves, you are slaves of the one whom you obey, either of sin, which leads to death, or of obedience, which leads to righteousness?

Commentary

After Jesus shared how to live for the Father's reward in spiritual disciplines, He transitioned and instructed how to live for the Father's reward in regard to our "treasures." Jesus gave two options to choose from as far as where our treasure is: on earth or in heaven; or as verse 24 clarifies, "God or money."

The word for money in this verse is "mammon." Matthew Henry explains, "Mammon … signifies gain; so that whatever in this world is, or is accounted by us to be gain is mammon." Our version of "gain" could be any manner of earthly treasure: success, riches, comfort, wealth, etc. Jesus urged His followers not to look for treasure in earthly gain but in God their Father who truly satisfies and meets every need.

Verse 19-21

Jesus tells us we are to "store up" treasure. To "store up" implies we are working for it and saving it for future use. It's an ongoing action that is reflected in our lifestyle. He addressed the durability of each type of treasure. Treasure on earth can be destroyed or stolen; its fleeting. Treasure in heaven is eternal and completely durable. It cannot be taken from us.

In Psalm 73:25, Asaph, speaking to God, said, "Whom have I in heaven but you? And there is nothing on earth I desire besides you, my flesh and my heart may fail, But God is the strength of my heart and my portion forever." Our heavenly treasure is God Himself. If we know Christ, He has secured this for us. Our heavenly treasure is "imperishable, undefiled and unfading, kept in heaven for [us]" (1 Peter 1:4). It can never be destroyed or stolen; nothing can separate us from Him. So, simply put, to store up treasure in heaven, we practice habits that help us to love God more and help others to love God more.

We delight in God's word, pursue obedience out of love for God, and we handle our treasure in a way that proves that our joy and pleasure is found in God. This earth will pass away, but He is forever.

We store up treasure in heaven because our heart will follow our treasure. The Message paraphrases verse 21, "...the place where your treasure is the place you most want to be."

Later in the gospel of Matthew, Jesus would speak with a rich young ruler who expressed his desire to enter the Kingdom of heaven. But when Jesus challenged him saying, "sell what you possess and give to the poor, and you will have treasure in heaven," it was revealed that his aim was to store up treasure on earth; he chose to keep his earthly treasure and not follow Jesus. Wherever our treasure is, our heart, perspective, and lifestyle will follow. Jesus expands on this in the next verses.

Verse 22

The treasure we seek affects our vision and perspective. Our eyes are the lamp of the body; what we see or focus on affects our perspective of faith. The healthy eye is not distracted, trying to focus on two opposite treasures at once. Our eyes should have a single focus, fixed on treasure in heaven that it may be a light to our vision and priorities. If your eye is healthy, focused on heaven, your body and faith will be full of light.

If your eye is bad, then your body will be full of darkness. Jesus was saying that a focus on earthly treasure corrupts the rest of our vision, hindering us from seeing things as they truly are. It results in distracted focus or double-vision and causes us to walk blindly and unwisely, chasing treasure of the world that will never satisfy. "If then the light in you is darkness, how great is the darkness?"

Verse 23-24

Finally, the place we store our treasure will affect who we serve. Jesus tells us we have to make a choice: treasure on earth or treasure in heaven; no one can serve two masters. In attempting to serve both God and earthly gain, you will, "love the one and hate the other, or be devoted to one and despise the other." Serving God or 'mammon' is not like employees working for employers, having two part-time jobs. The nature of serving God is all encompassing, your whole life is to be devoted to Him. In serving God, if another "master" requires something, you will resent it, "despise it and hate it." Conversely, if you are serving 'mammon' (money, status, success, etc.) as your master, devoting all your time and energy towards it, God's commands will just seem like a frustrating distraction to you.

Henry thoughtfully continues in his explanation, "*God* says, *'My son, give me thy heart.'* *Mammon* says, 'No, give it me.' *God* says, *'Be content with such things as ye have.'* *Mammon* says, 'Grasp at all that ever thou canst'. ... *God* says, 'Defraud not, never lie, be honest and just in all thy dealings.' *Mammon* says 'Cheat thine own Father, if thou canst gain by it.' *God* says, 'Be charitable.' *Mammon* says, 'Hold thy own: this giving undoes us all.' *God* says, *'Be careful for nothing.'* *Mammon* says, 'Be careful for every thing.' *God* says, *'Keep holy thy sabbath-day.'* *Mammon* says, 'Make use of that day as well as any other for the world.' Thus inconsistent are the commands of *God and Mammon,* so that we *cannot serve* both. Let us not then *halt between God and Baal, but choose ye this day whom ye will serve,* and abide by our choice."

We cannot serve God and money; their competing demands will not allow us to. We have to choose. Jesus was clear that to serve God for His treasure is the wise, obedient choice; the only one for the children of God.

Application & Reflection

1.What are your hopes and ambitions pertaining to 'treasure'? Is there an area where your treasure is in the wrong place?

2. Reflect on a time when you tried to serve "God and Money" at the same time. Why is this so impossible to do?

What did you learn about God from this experience?

3. Read **1 Timothy 6:9-19** and consider the following questions.

[9] But those who desire to be rich fall into temptation, into a snare, into many senseless and harmful desires that plunge people into ruin and destruction. [10] For the love of money is a root of all kinds of evils. It is through this craving that some have wandered away from the faith and pierced themselves with many pangs.

[11] But as for you, O man of God, flee these things. Pursue righteousness, godliness, faith, love, steadfastness, gentleness.[12] Fight the good fight of the faith. Take hold of the eternal life to which you were called and about which you made the good confession in the presence of many witnesses. [13] I charge you in the presence of God, who gives life to all things, and of Christ Jesus, who in his testimony before Pontius Pilate made the good confession,[14] to keep the commandment unstained and free from reproach until the appearing of our Lord Jesus Christ, [15] which he will display at the proper time—he who is the blessed and only Sovereign, the King of kings and Lord of lords, [16] who alone has

immortality, who dwells in unapproachable light, whom no one has ever seen or can see. To him be honor and eternal dominion. Amen.

[17] As for the rich in this present age, charge them not to be haughty, nor to set their hopes on the uncertainty of riches, but on God, who richly provides us with everything to enjoy. [18] They are to do good, to be rich in good works, to be generous and ready to share, [19] thus storing up treasure for themselves as a good foundation for the future, so that they may take hold of that which is truly life.

How can we increase our desire for treasure in heaven?

How can we store up treasure in heaven?

Lesson 11
The Treasure of the Family of God
Matthew 6:25–34

Observation & Interpretation

Read Matthew 6:25–34 and consider the following questions.

[25] "Therefore I tell you, do not be anxious about your life, what you will eat or what you will drink, nor about your body, what you will put on. Is not life more than food, and the body more than clothing?[26] Look at the birds of the air: they neither sow nor reap nor gather into barns, and yet your heavenly Father feeds them. Are you not of more value than they? [27] And which of you by being anxious can add a single hour to his span of life? [28] And why are you anxious about clothing? Consider the lilies of the field, how they grow: they neither toil nor spin, [29] yet I tell you, even Solomon in all his glory was not arrayed like one of these. [30] But if God so clothes the grass of the field, which today is alive and tomorrow is thrown into the oven, will he not much more clothe you, O you of little faith? [31] Therefore do not be anxious, saying, 'What shall we eat?' or 'What shall we drink?' or 'What shall we wear?' [32] For the Gentiles seek after all these things, and your heavenly Father knows that you need them all. [33] But seek first the kingdom of God and his righteousness, and all these things will be added to you.

[34] "Therefore do not be anxious about tomorrow, for tomorrow will be anxious for itself. Sufficient for the day is its own trouble.

1. Verse 25 begins with "Therefore," indicating a transition from the previous verses. How does the fact that our treasure is in heaven help us "not to be anxious"?

2. Describe Jesus' statement to not worry about the following in your own words:

Your life (25)

Food (26)

Clothing (28-30)

3. How do you think seeking and desiring God's kingdom first, and the corresponding promise, (Matthew 6:33) is an antidote for worry?

Commentary

Jesus convinced us in verses 1-24 that in all areas of life, including our spiritual disciplines and storing of treasure, the child of God's reward is in heaven. In verses 25-34, He explained how that perspective should influence our faith. These verses provide a wave of relief to an anxious heart as they reflect on God's Fatherly care. They also provide a challenge to have faith; for when our treasure is in heaven, we can trust our Father.

Verse 25

Jesus assumes we have chosen the wise, more durable treasure mentioned in 19-24 and then concludes, "Therefore, do not be anxious about your life." He is talking about the cares of life such as food and clothing. He said, "is not life more than food and the body more than clothing?" Our Father has taken care of our greatest need in turning us from enemies to sons and daughters. He has secured our treasure in heaven. Jesus came that we might have true, full life (John 10:10). If God has taken care of these things for us, how much more is He able to provide for food and clothing? For, "Is not life more than food and the body more than clothing?" (25)

Verse 26

Then Jesus told them to look at nature to gain an understanding of God's gracious provision. "Look at the birds..." The birds don't work for or store up their food. Our Father feeds them, though, He is not their Father, He is our Father. If He feeds the birds, how much more will He feed His own children? We are more valuable to God than birds.

Verse 27

Jesus added, "And which one of you by being anxious will add a single hour to his span of life?" The obvious answer is no one. Worry is a harmful, fruitless exercise. None of us can add a single hour, a single meal, or a single piece of clothing to our lives by worrying. Our lives are completely in our Father's sovereign and loving care.

Verses 28-30

Next, He addressed clothing. Again, He breaks through anxious thinking by suggesting a rational exercise in looking at nature, "consider the lilies…" Just like the birds, the lilies don't work for their clothing or spin their own thread, they just grow. But God clothes them with beauty for His glory. Solomon's wealth and glory were well known to all in that time. Jesus explained that God clothes the lilies with a splendor and glory greater than Solomon's. Then He concluded: if God clothes these lilies, "the grass," which will pass away… how much more will He clothe you? We are eternal beings who have God as our Father; He loves to bestow His glory on His children. Of course He will provide for us. Then Jesus gives a piercing diagnosis to worry when He says, "O you of little faith." Worrying about earthly treasure reflects an unbelief in God's kind, gracious, all-powerful providence. We must have faith in our Father's care.

Verses 31-34

Jesus concluded with a practical solution. We are not to worry about earthly treasure or what we will "eat, drink, or wear." The Gentiles seek these things, but the Gentiles do not have God as their Father. We have a heavenly Father who knows exactly what we need before we even ask. Instead, we are to seek His Kingdom first.

We seek His Kingdom as we treasure God's blessing (Matthew 5:3-12), God's approval (Matt 6:1), God's glory (Matt 5:16), God's righteousness (Matt 5:6, 6:33), and God's treasure (Matt 6:19-21). With this durable, eternal Kingdom in view, we will begin to prioritize correctly, and seek His Kingdom first. Then, God will make "his kingdom come" through us, for His glory and our good; and, also, "all these things," or our "daily bread," will be added to us.

"Therefore, do not be anxious about tomorrow, for tomorrow will be anxious for itself." Seeking the Kingdom happens one day at a time; with grace new each morning for every day. We are not to anxiously occupy our minds with the future but practice daily faithfulness and trust our Father for daily bread and daily grace.

Application & Reflection

1. How does your adoption into God's family help you choose Him as your treasure?

How does your adoption help you to trust Him for your needs?

2. Worrying can reveal where our heart's treasure is. Reflect on the things that cause you to worry. Is there something your heart is treasuring other than God?

3. How can you practically "seek the kingdom of God and His righteousness" as a way to pursue obedience to God and trust in His care?

4. How will the ambition of seeking God's Kingdom first inform the way you pray?

Lesson 12
Trusting God as our Father and Judge
Matthew 7:1-6

Observation and Interpretation

Read Matthew 7:1-6 and consider the following questions.

[1]"Judge not, that you be not judged. [2] For with the judgment you pronounce you will be judged, and with the measure you use it will be measured to you. [3] Why do you see the speck that is in your brother's eye, but do not notice the log that is in your own eye? [4] Or how can you say to your brother, 'Let me take the speck out of your eye,' when there is the log in your own eye? [5] You hypocrite, first take the log out of your own eye, and then you will see clearly to take the speck out of your brother's eye.

[6] "Do not give dogs what is holy, and do not throw your pearls before pigs, lest they trample them underfoot and turn to attack you.

1. In verses 1-2, why did Jesus command not to judge?

2. What metaphor did Jesus use to describe our sin in comparison with our brother's sin?

What do you think is meant by this?

3. According to verse 5, what are we to do before we confront a brother or sister regarding their sin?

4. Read **2 Peter 2:22** and **Revelation 22:14-15**. Considering these passages references to "dogs" and "pigs," who do you think Jesus was referring to in Matthew 7:6?

22 What the true proverb says has happened to them: "The dog returns to its own vomit, and the sow, after washing herself, returns to wallow in the mire."

14 Blessed are those who wash their robes, so that they may have the right to the tree of life and that they may enter the city by the gates. 15 Outside are the dogs and sorcerers and the sexually immoral and murderers and idolaters, and everyone who loves and practices falsehood.

5. Read **Matthew 10:11-15** and **Proverbs 9:7-8** and consider: how does this additional teaching help you understand Jesus' warning in Matthew 7:6?

[11] And whatever town or village you enter, find out who is worthy in it and stay there until you depart. [12] As you enter the house, greet it. [13] And if the house is worthy, let your peace come upon it, but if it is not worthy, let your peace return to you. [14] And if anyone will not receive you or listen to your words, shake off the dust from your feet when you leave that house or town. [15] Truly, I say to you, it will be more bearable on the day of judgment for the land of Sodom and Gomorrah than for that town.

[7] Whoever corrects a scoffer gets himself abuse,
  and he who reproves a wicked man incurs injury.
[8] Do not reprove a scoffer, or he will hate you;
  reprove a wise man, and he will love you.

Commentary

As Jesus continues to teach us how to live as disciples in His family, He transitions to teach how we should relate with our brothers and sisters. When we strive to imitate our Father's holiness, we will inevitably fail to measure up to the standard. We will also surely notice when our brothers and sisters fail to measure up. How should we treat our fellow brothers and sisters when this happens? How should we confront them?

Verse 1

His first instruction was, "Judge not, that you be not judged." When we see sin in the lives of other Christians, we are not to judge as if we are God. Just as in families with young children, siblings may try to take on the parent's role, assert their little "authorities" and direct one another; we too, as siblings in God's family, tend to try to wrongly take on our Father's role. How much more is this true in the family of God? We do not know the hearts of our brothers and sisters like God our Father does.

Jesus is not asking us to be blind or ignorant of others' sin, but He is asking us to imitate our Father and be gracious and generous. God is the perfect Judge of all, and even He "will not constantly accuse us" (Psalm 103:9, NLT). Sinclair Ferguson said, "The heart that has tasted the forgiveness of God will always be restrained in its judgement of others" (Akin, 122). Our Father is patient and gracious with us, and as we recall and reflect on His kindness in our lives, we are to be patient and gracious with our brothers and sisters.

Verse 2

Jesus explained, "For the judgement with which you pronounce you will be judged, and the measure you use will be measured to you." Paul explained this concept in Romans 2:1, saying, "...you have no excuse, O man, every one of you who judges. For in passing judgement on another you condemn yourself, because you, the judge, practice the very same things." When we take on the role of judge, we cannot pretend to be ignorant of the law that we claim to be able to administer to others (Stott, 177). We will be held accountable for the sins we judge others for and for the way we have judged.

Verse 3

Next Jesus gave an illustration on how our judgement may play out. First, He deals with our thoughts, "Why do you see the speck that is in your brother's eye, when there is a log in your own eye." Having a log in your eye would surely obstruct your vision, there is no way you could see or evaluate someone else's speck.

Jesus is saying: before you look at another's sin, evaluate yourself. Are you able to see clearly? Have you examined your own spiritual vision? The person in this metaphor was judgmental over someone else's sin when the sin in his own life kept him from being able to see clearly. Even though his was a "log," he still viewed his condition as more favorable than his brother's "speck."

Verse 4

This verse explains a situation where the judgmental brother actually tries to confront another brother in order to remove the "speck." "Or how can you *say* to your brother, 'Let me get the speck out of your eye.' When there is a log in your own eye." Obviously, if you have a log obstructing your vision, you are not at all capable of removing something from someone else's eye. It would only cause harm and more damage. It is the same with confronting someone's sin. When our sin has blinded us, we are not able to wisely confront a brother or sister.

Verse 5

Finally, Jesus gave the solution. First, He diagnosed the judgmental brother's problem with a word we have seen before. "You hypocrite..." The root of the issue with this hypocrite is he is acting one way on the outside, when he is completely different on the inside. He acts as if he is righteous on his own and capable of discerning and judging others—but, in reality, his pride and glaring sin are blocking his capability to love his brother. Akin explains, "Inspection of others without introspection of myself is the road to playing the hypocrite" (Akin, 124).

The solution? "First get the log out of your own eye." We are to examine ourselves and ask God to search us and know us and see if there is anything in our hearts that offends Him (Psalm 139:23-24). There *is* a need for us to confront one another regarding sin, but we are to do it, not as a hypocritical judge, but as a loving sibling and only after repentance over our own sin. After we experience repentance, we will "see clearly." We are to recognize our need for mercy and become poor in spirit. Then we can be merciful and be a peacemaker toward our brother or sister (Matthew 5:4,3,7). Then and only then will we be able to humbly go to our brother or sister to speak the truth in love and by God's grace, "take the speck our of [our] brother's eye."

Verse 6

Next Jesus gave a warning, and He shared how we should relate to someone or confront someone who is hostile toward the gospel. In this day, dogs traveled in packs and were aggressive towards people; they were vicious and dangerous. Pigs were ceremonially "unclean" animals and are never spoken of positively in scripture. "Dogs and pigs," were often used as labels in scripture for false teachers or people who openly rejected the gospel. Jesus warned, "Do not give to dogs what is holy or cast your pearls before pigs."

Dogs and pigs will not discern the precious value of a pearl, they would just trample over it or attack you. People hostile toward the good news of Jesus will not value it; they might even "turn to attack you." The book of Proverbs also warns of the danger and folly of rebuking a "scoffer" (Proverbs 9:7-8). Though we are to love and share Christ with all, if the message is repeatedly rejected, we are to move on. We can trust God's sovereignty as we share the truth. If we are met with hostility or an attack, we do not need to persist in offering "what is holy." Jesus' example is the best commentary on His teaching. In Matthew 10:11-15, Jesus instructed His disciples to share the news about the Kingdom of God, and if the message was rejected, they were to move on to the next town.

Application & Reflection

1. Do you view your own sin as more or less serious than the sin of other believers?

2. Jesus warns us to deal with our own hearts as much as we can before confronting a brother or sister. How might this instruction inform your prayer life?

3. How can understanding God as our perfect Father and Judge help us use discernment before confronting a brother or sister in Christ?

4. What are some ways we can use discernment before confronting someone who is hostile toward the Gospel?

Lesson 13
Coming to Our Father in Prayer
Matthew 7:7–12

Observation & Interpretation

Read Matthew 7:7–12 and consider the following questions.

[7] "Ask, and it will be given to you; seek, and you will find; knock, and it will be opened to you. [8] For everyone who asks receives, and the one who seeks finds, and to the one who knocks it will be opened. [9] Or which one of you, if his son asks him for bread, will give him a stone? [10] Or if he asks for a fish, will give him a serpent? [11] If you then, who are evil, know how to give good gifts to your children, how much more will your Father who is in heaven give good things to those who ask him!

[12] "So whatever you wish that others would do to you, do also to them, for this is the Law and the Prophets.

1. Describe the nature of the "asking" in verses 7 and 8 in your own words.

2. What do verses 7-11 tell us about the character of God and the way we should relate to Him in prayer?

3. Read **Luke 11:11-13**, **Matthew 6:33,** and **John 15:7**.

¹¹ What father among you, if his son asks for a fish, will instead of a fish give him a serpent; ¹² or if he asks for an egg, will give him a scorpion? ¹³ If you then, who are evil, know how to give good gifts to your children, how much more will the heavenly Father give the Holy Spirit to those who ask him!"

³³ But seek first the kingdom of God and his righteousness, and all these things will be added to you.

⁷ If you abide in me, and my words abide in you, ask whatever you wish, and it will be done for you.

Considering these verses and the Sermon on Mount as a whole, what kind of prayers do you think Jesus encouraged us to pray in Matthew 7:7-11?

4. Describe a few ways you think "the Law and the Prophets" and, specifically, Jesus' explanation of the law in Matthew 5:17-7:12 are "summed" up in Matthew 7:12.

How do you think this connects to the application given in verse 13?

Commentary

As Jesus brings His teaching to a close, the weightiness of the task before the disciples is heavy. Jesus wanted them to know that when their calling feels burdensome (or any other time) they, like free and bold children, can come to their good Father in prayer.

Verses 7 and 8

Jesus explained in several ways that our Father desires for us to come to Him in prayer. "Ask and you will receive; seek and you will find; knock and it will be opened to you." God is ready to hear and listen. We are to come to Him as a child comes to his Father: free, persistent, and bold. He is honored by our dependency and our childlike requests; He loves when we talk to Him.

For, "everyone who asks, receives and whoever seeks finds and whoever knocks it will be opened to him," Jesus makes a promise that everyone who comes to Him in prayer will be heard and will receive from God.

Verses 9 and 10

What will they receive? Jesus explained by pointing us to an illustration of a father and child. The good father hears the son or daughter's requests; he does not ignore them. If a child asks for a fish, their father would never give them a serpent or something harmful. He delights in meeting the needs of his child.

Though we may have an idea of what a "good" father looks like, Jesus still puts all earthly fathers in the same category we are all in, "you who are evil." Even "evil" fathers are capable of giving good gifts to their children. So "how much more," Jesus says, "will your heavenly Father give good things to those who ask Him?"

Here Jesus explains that while some of us have an example of a good father who answers and gives to his children, even the good fathers we can think of have no comparison to the goodness of our Heavenly Father. (Some of us do not have an example of a good father. But Jesus' analogy is filled with hope; He offers grace and redemption for all kinds of earthly father examples.)

For, even good fathers fit the description in Paul's argument in Romans, they "would scarcely die for a righteous person-though perhaps for a good person one would dare to even die…" But God is an altogether set apart kind of Father. "God shows His love for us in this: that while we were still sinners, Christ died for us…" We can have hope in His goodness and generosity, because in order to make us sons and daughters, God, "did not spare his own Son, but graciously gave him up for us all, how will he not also with him graciously give us all things?" (Romans 5:7-8,10; 8:32)

This doesn't mean that God gives us whatever we ask for. It actually means something infinitely better and richer than that. Our limitedness and sin limit and taint our desires and perceived needs in various ways. So we may have foolish requests or requests that we think are good but are actually harmful— or requests that are good but that are only the best our finite minds can think of. But, no matter our requests, God in His limitless, all wise, perfect love and goodness will give us the best thing *He* can think of, according to His "good, pleasing and perfect will" (Romans 12:2). *The Author of good has promised to give us good things when we ask.*

Verse 11

After Jesus finishes helping us to reflect on God's goodness toward us, He shares how this should influence our goodness toward others. "So whatever you wish others would do to you, do also to them." This is known as the "Golden Rule." As we read in verses 7-10 (and the whole rest of the Sermon) our Father is the one who perfectly treats His children according to the Golden Rule. He, with perfect wisdom and an infinite knowledge of His children's hearts, knows how they would want to be treated. He gives and acts according to His goodness. Therefore, we should imitate our Father. We should think about how we would want to be treated, doing our best with God's help to discern good. Then we should treat others according to this good.

"This is the sum of the law and the prophets." Later Jesus would say this in a different way, "And he said to him, 'You shall love the Lord your God with all your heart and with all your soul and with all your mind. This is the great and first commandment. And a second is like it: You shall love your neighbor as yourself. On these two commandments depend all the Law and the Prophets'" (Matthew 22:37-40). When we stop to sincerely think "how would I want to be treated in this situation?" We "love our neighbor as ourselves." Application of the "Golden Rule" is a way we can pursue obedience to God.

Application & Reflection

1. Read **Romans 8:28-32** and reflect on God's generous fatherly care for you.

²⁸ And we know that for those who love God all things work together for good, for those who are called according to his purpose. ²⁹ For those whom he foreknew he also predestined to be conformed to the image of his Son, in order that he might be the firstborn among many brothers. ³⁰ And those whom he predestined he also called, and those whom he called he also justified, and those whom he justified he also glorified.

³¹ What then shall we say to these things? If God is for us, who can be against us? ³² He who did not spare his own Son but gave him up for us all, how will he not also with him graciously give us all things?

How does God's character as our Father encourage you to pursue the freedom and expectancy in prayer that Jesus describes?

2. As you reflect on God's character and His encouragement to pray, what are some prayers you think you should pray with more persistence?

What can you start praying this week?

3. How did Jesus exemplify the "Golden Rule" (verse 13)?

How can the fact that Jesus treats us according to the "Golden Rule" help us live by it as well?

Lesson 14
Choose the Way of the Kingdom
Matthew 7:13–23

Observation & Interpretation

Read Matthew 7:13–23 and consider the following questions.

13 "Enter by the narrow gate. For the gate is wide and the way is easy[a] that leads to destruction, and those who enter by it are many. 14 For the gate is narrow and the way is hard that leads to life, and those who find it are few.

15 "Beware of false prophets, who come to you in sheep's clothing but inwardly are ravenous wolves. 16 You will recognize them by their fruits. Are grapes gathered from thornbushes, or figs from thistles? 17 So, every healthy tree bears good fruit, but the diseased tree bears bad fruit. 18 A healthy tree cannot bear bad fruit, nor can a diseased tree bear good fruit. 19 Every tree that does not bear good fruit is cut down and thrown into the fire. 20 Thus you will recognize them by their fruits.

21 "Not everyone who says to me, 'Lord, Lord,' will enter the kingdom of heaven, but the one who does the will of my Father who is in heaven. 22 On that day many will say to me, 'Lord, Lord, did we not prophesy in your name, and cast out demons in your name, and do many mighty works in your name?' 23 And then will I declare to them, 'I never knew you; depart from me, you workers of lawlessness.'

1. As Jesus concludes, He calls His audience to a response. What is His challenge in verses 13-14?

2. Why do you think the warning about false prophets is mentioned right after Jesus' words about the "narrow gate" (13)?

3. Use your own words to explain how Jesus described the false prophets and how we are to recognize them.

4. Jesus gives another warning in Matthew 7:21-23. Read this along with **1 John 5:2-4**.

[2] By this we know that we love the children of God, when we love God and obey his commandments. [3] For this is the love of God, that we keep his commandments. And his commandments are not burdensome. [4] For everyone who has been born of God overcomes the world. And this is the victory that has overcome the world—our faith.

According to 1 John 5:2-3 and Matthew 7:21, what is the evidence of knowing and loving God?

5. According to Matthew 7:23, how does Jesus describe those who will not enter His Kingdom?

Commentary

Jesus had given His instructions for the new Kingdom, and as His sermon closes, He gives a call to respond. He challenged His disciples to enter the narrow gate of the Kingdom. In doing so, they were to be wary of false teachers and examine themselves to make sure they belonged to God.

Verses 13 and 14

He said, "enter by the narrow gate." Then He compares their two options. There is a narrow and a wide gate. The way of the wide gate is easy, but it leads to destruction.

In Psalm 73:4-9, the Psalmist provides vivid illustrations of the "life that leads to destruction" and its apparent ease:

"For they have no pangs until death;
   their bodies are fat and sleek.
They are not in trouble as others are;
   they are not stricken like the rest of mankind.
Therefore pride is their necklace;
   violence covers them as a garment.
Their eyes swell out through fatness;

   their hearts overflow with follies.
They scoff and speak with malice;
   loftily they threaten oppression.
They set their mouths against the heavens,
   and their tongue struts through the earth."

The wide way is the way of this world; it's choosing your treasure on earth. Though life through the wide gate appears easy, it only leads to destruction. Earthly treasure is temporary and fleeting.

Jesus already convinced us that the more valuable, durable treasure is in heaven. We have treasure in heaven when we choose the narrow, hard way that "leads to life." Psalm 73 concludes the same:

"Whom have I in heaven but you?
  And there is nothing on earth that I desire besides you.
 My flesh and my heart may fail,
  but God is the strength of my heart and my portion forever…
For behold, those who are far from you shall perish;
  you put an end to everyone who is unfaithful to you.
But for me it is good to be near God;
  I have made the Lord GOD my refuge,
  that I may tell of all your works."

Psalm 73: 2-26, 28-29

Choosing treasure in heaven, "life" in Christ, and nearness to God our Father requires the hard way. J. I Packer states it this way:

"In this world, royal children have to undergo extra training and discipline in which other children escape, in order to fit them for their high destiny. It is the same with the children of the King of kings. The clue to understanding all his dealings with them is to remember that throughout their lives he is training them for what awaits them, and chiseling them into the image of Christ." (Knowing God, 222)

God's children are called to be separate, as God prepares us to live with Him as our treasure for eternity. Jesus urges us to choose this narrow way that leads to life.

Verse 15-20

How do we go about choosing this narrow way? Jesus gave us practical instructions. First, "Beware of false prophets, who come to you in sheep's clothing but inwardly are ravenous wolves."

Jeremiah describes an example of a false prophet:

"Do not listen to the words of prophets who prophesy to you, filling you with vain hopes. They speak visions of their own minds, not from the mouth of the Lord. They say continually to those who despise the word of the Lord, 'It shall be well with you'; and to everyone who stubbornly follows his own heart, they say, 'No disaster shall come upon you'" (Jeremiah 23:16-17).

The danger of the false prophets is that they come in "sheep's clothing" appearing innocent, telling people things that appeal to "itching ears" (2 Timothy 4:3), but they are dangerous like ravenous wolves. False teachers' aim is to deliberately lead others away from the truth of Jesus. We will recognize them by their "fruits." Just as a healthy tree cannot bear bad fruit and a diseased tree cannot bear good fruit, teachers filled with the Holy Spirit will have fruit of truth and fruits of the spirit (Galatians 5:22-23) pointing to Jesus. False prophets will produce fruit that may sound appealing, "filling with hope," but over time that hope will prove vain.

So, the first application in choosing the way of the Kingdom is to be on guard against false teaching. Know what the truth is and be able to discern when you are being told a lie. A teacher's life, conduct, character, and the evidence or lack of evidence of the Holy Spirit will be the fruit we can discern in examining their influence. The wide way is appealing, easy, and with the appearance that "no disaster shall come." But in reality, the wide way leads to destruction.

Verses 21-23

Jesus gave more instruction on how to know if you are on the narrow way, and how to know if you truly belong to Him. When Jesus returns, many will call Him "Lord" with their lips. These people will appear to have done "many mighty works" in the name of Jesus, and they will appeal to Him based on those works.

In verse 23, Jesus says He will declare to those with only lip service and outward acts, "I never knew you, depart from me you workers of lawlessness." The people in verse 23 have an outward profession of faith, and they do many good works in the name of Jesus. But Jesus still calls them "lawless," because they have not dealt with the sin in their hearts. John expands on the concept of lawlessness: "Everyone who makes a practice of sinning also practices lawlessness; sin is lawlessness. You know that he appeared in order to take away sins, and in him there is no sin. No one who abides in him keeps on sinning; no one who keeps on sinning has either seen him or known him" (1 John 3:4-6).

In order to know Jesus, we need Him to take away our sin. As we have already studied, the one who enters the Kingdom is the one who appeals to God based only on Christ's work and mercy, crying out, "have mercy on me, a sinner." God grants this poverty in spirit, not when we give mere lip service and outward works to Him, but when we depend on Christ's righteousness and our adoption through the Holy Spirit. Then and only then, He removes our "lawlessness," and we will "know" Jesus our brother, and God our Father.

Our belonging to Him will be evident by our "doing His will" or obeying His word. To know Him is to love Him, and to love Him is to obey Him. Our belonging to the family of God is marked by our obedience to our Father.

Application & Reflection

1. How have you experienced that "the way is narrow and hard that leads to life"?

2. Read **Psalm 73:18-28**.

Truly you set them in slippery places;
    you make them fall to ruin.
19 How they are destroyed in a moment,
    swept away utterly by terrors!
20 Like a dream when one awakes,
    O Lord, when you rouse yourself, you despise them as phantoms.
21 When my soul was embittered,
    when I was pricked in heart,
22 I was brutish and ignorant;
    I was like a beast toward you.
23 Nevertheless, I am continually with you;
    you hold my right hand.
24 You guide me with your counsel,
    and afterward you will receive me to glory.
25 Whom have I in heaven but you?
    And there is nothing on earth that I desire besides you.
26 My flesh and my heart may fail,
    but God is the strength[b] of my heart and my portion forever.
27 For behold, those who are far from you shall perish;
    you put an end to everyone who is unfaithful to you.
28 But for me it is good to be near God;
    I have made the Lord God my refuge,
    that I may tell of all your works.

How can the realization in Psalm 73:23-28 help us to choose the difficult path leading to life?

3. Sometimes, false teachers will use scripture. How will we know whether a teacher is using scripture correctly or deceptively?

What can you do this week to prepare and guard yourself against false teaching?

4. Considering Matthew 7:21-23, how can you be certain that Jesus knows you?

What steps could a person, alongside their church, take to make sure they are known by Jesus?

Lesson 15 and Conclusion
A Call to Obedience
Matthew 7:24-29

Observation & Interpretation

Read Matthew 7:24-29 and consider the following questions.

²⁴ "Everyone then who hears these words of mine and does them will be like a wise man who built his house on the rock. ²⁵ And the rain fell, and the floods came, and the winds blew and beat on that house, but it did not fall, because it had been founded on the rock. ²⁶ And everyone who hears these words of mine and does not do them will be like a foolish man who built his house on the sand. ²⁷ And the rain fell, and the floods came, and the winds blew and beat against that house, and it fell, and great was the fall of it."

²⁸ And when Jesus finished these sayings, the crowds were astonished at his teaching, ²⁹ for he was teaching them as one who had authority, and not as their scribes.

1. Describe the similarities and differences between the two builders Jesus described.

2. Read Luke's account of this teaching in **Luke 6:46-49** and consider: how do you think Matthew 7:24-29 is connected to Matthew 7:21-23?

[46] "Why do you call me 'Lord, Lord,' and not do what I tell you? [47] Everyone who comes to me and hears my words and does them, I will show you what he is like: [48] he is like a man building a house, who dug deep and laid the foundation on the rock. And when a flood arose, the stream broke against that house and could not shake it, because it had been well built. [49] But the one who hears and does not do them is like a man who built a house on the ground without a foundation. When the stream broke against it, immediately it fell, and the ruin of that house was great."

3. According to Matthew 5:29, what was the difference between the teaching of the scribes and the teaching of Jesus?

4. When Jesus finished teaching, what was the reaction of the crowds?

Commentary

In the previous verses, Jesus explained that the one who knows Him is the one who obeys Him and does "the will of the Father." As He concludes, He explains how knowing Him determines the result of the "storm" of judgement. Through an illustration of two builders and two houses, Jesus told His audience that the house or life that will "stand in the judgement" (Psalm 1:5) is the one whose foundation is knowing Him and obeying His word.

Verses 24-27

The two builders both heard the words of Jesus. They both built a house, and both houses were exposed to the same storm. The wise man heard the words of Jesus and put them into practice; he built his house on the rock. When exposed to the wind and rain, the house was able to stand on its strong, rock foundation. The foolish man heard the words of Jesus and did not put them into practice; he built his house on the sand. When the storm came, his house fell, "and great was its fall."

The builders represent hearers of the word. Both of them heard Jesus' words. In this context, the words Jesus is referring to is the teaching of the Sermon on the Mount. Each man responded to the teaching differently—one chose to obey and "put them into practice," the other did not. The one who listened built his life on the foundation of God's word, knowing Christ. The other ignored God's words and decided to build his life based on his own ideas.

Storms were often used to symbolize judgement throughout the Old Testament. Jeremiah 23:19-20 says:

"Behold, the storm of the LORD!
  Wrath has gone forth,
 a whirling tempest;
  it will burst upon the head of the wicked.
The anger of the LORD will not turn back
  until he has executed and accomplished
  the intents of his heart.
In the latter days you will understand it clearly."

Digging through the sand to find a rock foundation is hard; it is easier to build the walls of the house without concern for the foundation. In the same way, it can be tempting to go through life carelessly, not considering motives or "foundations," and just pursuing productivity and enjoyment for productivity and enjoyment's sake. For a while, the houses and lives may look similar; nobody will know the difference. But when "the rains fall and the floods come," only the house built on the rock and the life built on knowing Christ will stand. As John Rippon, the hymn writer said, "How firm a foundation, ye saints of the Lord, is laid for your faith in His excellent word! What more can He say than to you He hath said, to you who for refuge to Jesus have fled?" Jesus is our refuge and strength, our strong foundation.

Jesus ended the sermon on a somber note, with the image of a house falling with a "great fall." The audience was meant to be left with something to deeply consider, and so are we. What is your life built on? Is it your own effort, or is it the Holy Spirit in you? Your opinions and ideas, or God's truthful word? Your own reputation, or your poverty in spirit and need for mercy? Your knowledge of scripture, or knowing Christ to whom the scriptures point?

To the one who builds his life on the foundation of Jesus, their life will stand through the storm of judgment. When we trust in Christ's righteousness as given to us through the cross, we are secure in God's family. Nothing will ever separate us from our Father.

Verse 29

Lastly, Matthew recorded the response of the crowds. When Jesus finished, the crowds were "astonished." Why? Because Jesus taught as one who had authority. As the Author of the word, Christ alone had the authority to teach the way He did. Unlike their scribes, Jesus didn't teach a second-hand message, He taught with authority the law that He had come to fulfill.

Jesus perfectly fulfills the Sermon on the Mount. He is characterized by the traits and blessings of God in the Beatitudes (Matthew 5:3-12). He is the light of the world, and the one who not only preserves the earth as salt does, but He is making all things new through the power of His resurrection (Matthew 5:13-16). He fulfilled the righteous requirements of the law by obedience to His Father from His heart. He then, in turn, grants us new hearts by His Holy Spirit (Matthew 5:17-48). He lived a life in perfect fellowship with His Father in His spiritual disciplines; and He always loved, treasured, and trusted His Father above all else (Matthew 6). And though He is the Judge and ruler of all, He chooses humility and long-suffering toward our sins—as He constantly, persistently prays to the Father, interceding for us on our behalf (Matthew 7:1-12).

So, yes, Jesus taught with authority. In fact, "no one ever spoke like this man" (John 7:46). How will you respond? Jesus longs that we would not just be "astonished," but that we would be obedient.

Through His work on the cross, He has adopted us into His family, giving us His spirit so that we may live out the calling of the Sermon on the Mount (Romans 8:15-16). He has convinced us that living in obedience to this sermon is a life of deep blessing and intimate fellowship with Him. As we consider His words and live by His spirit, may we live out the Sermon on the Mount through the adoption Jesus bought for us—as sons and daughters of God.

Application & Reflection

1. Why is this passage a fitting way to end the Sermon on the Mount?

2. Think over this passage in the context of the whole Sermon on the Mount. Is there a specific area of His teaching you have heard (25) or been "astonished" by (29) but not obedient?

What steps could you take to be obedient to His words?

3. Read Romans 8:31-39 and reflect on the fact that Christ is our sure foundation. If we have trusted in Him, we have been adopted into the family of God forever.

[31] What then shall we say to these things? If God is for us, who can be against us? [32] He who did not spare his own Son but gave him up for us all, how will he not also with him graciously give us all things? [33] Who shall bring any charge against God's elect? It is God

who justifies. ³⁴ Who is to condemn? Christ Jesus is the one who died—more than that, who was raised—who is at the right hand of God, who indeed is interceding for us. ³⁵ Who shall separate us from the love of Christ? Shall tribulation, or distress, or persecution, or famine, or nakedness, or danger, or sword? ³⁶ As it is written,

"For your sake we are being killed all the day long;
   we are regarded as sheep to be slaughtered."

³⁷ No, in all these things we are more than conquerors through him who loved us. ³⁸ For I am sure that neither death nor life, nor angels nor rulers, nor things present nor things to come, nor powers, ³⁹ nor height nor depth, nor anything else in all creation, will be able to separate us from the love of God in Christ Jesus our Lord.

 How does God's love for us through the sure foundation of Christ spur you on as you seek to live out your position as a child of God?

Appendix
Christ-centered Repentance

A guide to practice Jesus' admonition:

"Repent, for the Kingdom of heaven is at hand." Matthew 4:17

The term "repentance" illustrates a "turning" from our own sinful way toward an obedience to God. Our hope in repentance is Christ:

"For our sake he made him to be sin who knew no sin, so that in him we might become the righteousness of God."
2 Corinthians 5:21

"If we claim to be without sin, we deceive ourselves and the truth is not in us. If we confess our sins, he is faithful and just and will forgive us our sins and purify us from all unrighteousness."
1 John 1:9

The way we pursue Christ's righteousness is through confession and repentance. Here are some practical suggestions for steps in repentance from Psalm 51.

1. Psalm 51:1: Appeal to God's mercy.
> "Have mercy on me, O God,
>   according to your steadfast love;
> according to your abundant mercy
>   blot out my transgressions"

We ask and appeal to God for mercy. We do not ask for mercy depending on our own asking or our own ability to do better or our own work or goodness. When we ask for forgiveness, we are fully dependent on God's great mercy toward us in Christ.

2. Psalm 51:2-3, 17: Name and acknowledge your sin.

" Wash me thoroughly from my iniquity,
   and cleanse me from my sin!
For I know my transgressions,
   and my sin is ever before me...
...The sacrifices of God are a broken spirit;
   a broken and contrite heart, O God, you will not despise."

Give an honest, full confession. He is not and will never be surprised by what you have to confess. Jesus "will never cast out" those who come to Him in repentance. (John 6:37). He gently, tenderly handles "broken and contrite" hearts (Psalm 51:17).

3. Psalm 51:4: Acknowledge your sin is against God

"Against you, you only, have I sinned
   and done what is evil in your sight,
so that you may be justified in your words
   and blameless in your judgment."

Though there are many good fruits of repentance, the primary aim in our repentance is to restore our fellowship with God. And for this, we must acknowledge that we have grieved Him with our sin. The root of our sin is always primarily against God. Our sin breaks God's rule, will, and law.

4. Psalm 51:7-10: Look to Jesus.

" Purge me with hyssop, and I shall be clean;
   wash me, and I shall be whiter than snow.
Let me hear joy and gladness;
   let the bones that you have broken rejoice.
Hide your face from my sins,
   and blot out all my iniquities.
[1] Create in me a clean heart, O God,
   and renew a right[spirit within me."

David asks repeatedly to be cleansed and washed from the weight and hard heartedness caused by sin. From the New Testament, we know this is possible because of Jesus. "... when the goodness and loving kindness of God our Savior appeared, he saved us, not because of the works done by us in righteousness, but according to His own mercy, by the washing of regeneration and renewal of the Holy Spirit, whom He poured out on us richly through Jesus Christ our Savior, so that being justified by His grace we might become heirs according to the hope of eternal life"(Titus 3:4). When we ask for cleansing from our sin, we can do it with confidence in the work of Christ.

5. Psalm 51:8-12: Receive God's healing, restoration, and the joy of salvation.

> "Let me hear joy and gladness;
>   let the bones that you have broken rejoice.
> Hide your face from my sins,
>   and blot out all my iniquities.
> Create in me a clean heart, O God,
>   and renew a right spirit within me.
> Cast me not away from your presence,
>   and take not your Holy Spirit from me.
> Restore to me the joy of your salvation,
>   and uphold me with a willing spirit."

Our sin and conviction often leave us broken in spirit. After repentance, we long for a "right spirit" to experience the joy of God's salvation and His presence. If we belong to Christ, we know the joy and blessed humility that comes with being loved, redeemed, and accepted by Him. God can remind us of our status in Christ, restore this joy to us, and uphold us with His spirit.

6. Psalm 51:13-16: Pray that God would use your forgiveness for His glory.

"Then I will teach transgressors your ways,
    and sinners will return to you.
Deliver me from bloodguiltiness, O God,
    O God of my salvation,
    and my tongue will sing aloud of your righteousness.
O Lord, open my lips,
    and my mouth will declare your praise.
For you will not delight in sacrifice, or I would give it;
    you will not be pleased with a burnt offering."

When we experience God's forgiveness, He gives us a desire to help others experience His grace and forgiveness as we have. We should decide to tell others of the grace and forgiveness we have received. "Lord, open my lips that my mouth might declare your praise."

7. Psalm 51:18-19: As you resolve to obey, ask God that He would protect the church and those around you from the effects of your sin.

"Do good to Zion in your good pleasure;
    build up the walls of Jerusalem;
then will you delight in right sacrifices,
    in burnt offerings and whole burnt offerings;
    then bulls will be offered on your altar."

After his repentance, David asks for worship to be restored in the temple. He was an influential person, and he knew his actions could have a ripple effect. When we learn about our sin, we should pray for the church. We are "members of one another" (Romans 12:4) and our actions affect one another.

Acknowledgements

To my husband, Philip Lee, whose steady, constant belief in me lends me the bravery I need to take steps of faithfulness. Thank you to Annie Kate Saunders at Meliora Word for her helpful edits. To the women of Redemption Hill Church, who graciously held me up with such generous encouragement. And to Jesus, the King... truly anything for Him.

Bibliography

1. Taken from the ESV® Study Bible (The Holy Bible, English Standard Version®), copyright ©2008 by Crossway, a publishing ministry of Good News Publishers. Used by permission. All rights reserved.

2. Unless otherwise noted: Scripture quotations are from the ESV® Bible (The Holy Bible, English Standard Version®), copyright © 2001 by Crossway, a publishing ministry of Good News Publishers. Used by permission. All rights reserved.

3. Scripture quotations marked MSG are taken from *THE MESSAGE*, copyright © 1993, 2002, 2018 by Eugene H. Peterson. Used by permission of NavPress. All rights reserved. Represented by Tyndale House Publishers, a Division of Tyndale House Ministries.

4. Scripture quotations marked (NLT) are taken from the Holy Bible, New Living Translation, copyright ©1996, 2004, 2015 by Tyndale House Foundation. Used by permission of Tyndale House Publishers, a Division of Tyndale House Ministries, Carol Stream, Illinois 60188. All rights reserved.

5. Henry, Matthew. Matthew Henry Commentary on the Whole Bible (Complete). Matthew, 1706. Available online at biblestudytools.com/commentaries/matthew-henry-complete/

6. Daniel L Akin, Christ-Centered Exposition Commentary: Exalting Jesus in the Sermon on the Mount. Copyright © 2019 Daniel L. Akin. Nashville, Tennessee. B&H Publishing Group. Reprinted and used by permission.

7. Packer, J.I, *Knowing God*. Downers Grove, IL: InterVarsity Press, 1993.

8. Stott, John. *The Message of the Sermon on the Mount.* Downers Grove, IL: InterVarsity Press, 1978.

9. *What is Righteousness?* (2020)
https://www.gotquestions.org/righteousness.html